Flavors of Lebanon

By Vera Shammas and Gail Shammas

OVER 130 AUTHENTIC ORIGINAL RECIPES
FROM NORTHERN LEBANON

AuthorHouse™
1663 Liberty Drive
Bloomington, IN 47403
www.authorhouse.com
Phone: 1 (800) 839-8640

Design & Layout by Emily S. Sutton

Published by AuthorHouse 02/06/2015

ISBN: 978-1-4969-6530-1 (sc)
ISBN: 978-1-4969-6825-8 (e)

Library of Congress Control Number: 2015901879

Contents

About the Authors

Vera Y Shammas (born 1935, Lebanon; naturalized US citizen) is a recent immigrant to the United States from Lebanon. As a homemaker, she has dedicated her life to her home and has developed and tested several hundred Lebanese dishes. In this book she shares with us the art of cooking some of the most popular and authentic meals known to her home country, particularly the North Lebanese Cuisine.

Gail Shammas on a camel in the Bekaa valley the main agricultural section of Lebanon.

Gail A Shammas, B.Sc, RN (born in 1962, USA) is a registered nurse. She obtained her Bachelor of Science in Nursing at the University Iowa Hospitals and Clinics in Iowa, USA. She is currently a Research Coordinator at the Midwest Cardiovascular Research Foundation in Davenport, Iowa. She has co-authored several scientific publications in the health field. Gail has traveled to Lebanon a few times with her husband, Dr. Nicolas Shammas, a native of Amyoun, Lebanon. She has developed a special interest in ethnic cooking. She has made the recipes in this book easy to duplicate using accurate western measures.

Thank You

In memory of my beloved husband
Wahib Nicolas Shammas and to my
children Nicolas, Robert, Claudette
and Diana and their families

Vera Shammas

To my husband Nicolas for all his
support and love, and to my wonderful
children Waheeb John, Andrew Nicolas
and Anna Elizabeth
So they enjoy these recipes
for years to come and share them with
their children and grandchildren

Gail Shammas

Introduction

St John church, a Crusader's church (1099-1100) built over a 28 man-made crypts from the Phoenician's time in Amyoun, North of Lebanon where Vera Shammas resides. Amyoun or Amyun may be considered one of the oldest towns in Lebanon. The name has semitic origin and means the "tough and firm fortress". In Aramaic (Am Yuwn) it means the Greek People. Amyoun is the capital of the predominantly Greek Orthodox area Koura District.

Cedars of North Lebanon. Thousands of years old, these trees have been mentioned in the Old Testament in the Psalms of Solomon 92:12 "The righteous shall flourish like the palm tree and grow like a cedar in Lebanon". The cedar tree is also at the center of the Lebanese flag.

"Flavors of Lebanon" is a collection of recipes from the Northern part of Lebanon and an expansion of the previously published first edition "Flavors of Lebanon" by the same authors.

I was born in the beautiful town of Amyoun (pictured on the next page), in North Lebanon. Like many homes in our village, families and friends frequently get together to talk, drink, and enjoy great Lebanese food. My mother, Vera Shammas, known for her authentic Lebanese cooking was known as a "master cook" and quite often the cooking resource for the neighborhood ladies. Her recipes have been handed down to her from her mother and grandmother. She has expanded them with her cooking mastery, and they have become popular in our town among our family and friends. These recipes are truly a treasure that I have cherished all my life. As she comes often to visit me in the United States after I have immigrated to Iowa over 24 years ago, her recipes have remained the same and have always brought the best memory of my childhood. These delicious meals have been cooked with pride and reflected the richness of a culture existing in a small world that has been a crossroad for many civilizations and a mosaic of different customs and flavors. I was fortunate to see my wife, Gail, taking a deep interest in the North Lebanese cuisine. With a nursing background and a love for healthy food, Gail spent countless hours with my mom Vera learning her recipes and writing them in ways that can be duplicated using western measures.

"Flavors of Lebanon" is a collection of these recipes that Vera Shammas and Gail Shammas share with us with passion and pride. These are the same authentic recipes that I grew up feasting on when I was a kid in Amyoun and now they are yours too to enjoy!

This book clearly brings to those who are seeking genuine Lebanese cuisine the food of the North of Lebanon. It should be noted that the food across Lebanon is mostly the same despite subtle variations in its preparation. You will always find the famous mezza, a selection of 60 or more different appetizers; tabouli, the delicious and satisfying Lebanese salad; kibbi, made of ground meat and Burghul (crushed wheat) in various gourmet dishes; laban (yogurt) meals and so forth that make the Lebanese cuisine a truly unique and enjoyable experience. Lebanese dishes are easy to prepare and are made easier in this book using standard western measures. Furthermore, little is known about the nutritional aspect of Lebanese cooking which we provide to our readers. The carbohydrate, protein, fat and cholesterol contents in every meal were determined using various scientific references. The nutritional information provided will prove to be valuable to those eagerly interested in health food. Computations performed in this book are only approximations.

I am confident that you will enjoy these wonderful and authentic recipes that will transcend you to the North of Lebanon and get you one step closer to one of the oldest and richest cultures on earth. Bon Appetite!

Nicolas W. Shammas, MD, EJD, MS

The Sajj (pictured right) is a round metal griddle in the shape of a convex dome that allows baking of large diameter flatbreads called marqouq. Making of large flatbread is not discussed in this book but it is not infrequent to see this in bakery stores in Lebanon.

Breads

Basic Bread Dough
(ajeen khubz)

SERVES 6 | 264 calories per serving

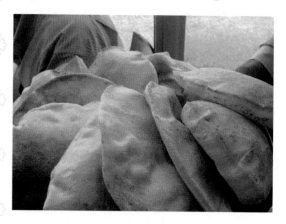

1 cup	lukewarm water, divided
2 teaspoons	dry active yeast
2 teaspoons	sugar
3 cups	plus 2 teaspoons flour, divided
1 teaspoon	salt

Mix 1/2 cup of lukewarm water, yeast, sugar and 2 teaspoons of flour well. Allow 10 minutes for yeast mix to rise. In a food processor place remaining flour, 1/2 cup of water, salt and yeast mix. Process for few minutes. If needed, add slowly additional lukewarm water or flour while processing until dough is firm. Remove dough from processor and knead on a floured board with both hands for a few minutes. Cover dough and allow rising for 2 hours in a warm place. Split dough into 6 equal pieces. Roll each piece on a floured board into 1/8 inch thick circles using a rolling pin.vCover circles with cloth and let sit for 1 hour. Preheat oven to 500°F. Place dough on a baking sheet in oven until bread rises (approximately 3-4 minutes).

Estimated time of preparation/baking: 1 hour

Pie Dough
(ajeen ftayer)

SERVES 6 | 429 calories per serving

1 cup	lukewarm water, divided
2 1/4 teaspoons	dry active yeast or 1 packet yeast
1/2 teaspoon	sugar
3 cups	flour
1/2 cup	olive oil
1 teaspoon	salt

Mix 1/2 cup lukewarm water, yeast and sugar. Allow 5-10 minutes for yeast mix to proof or foam and bubble. In a food processor or stand mixer add flour, oil, salt and yeast mix. Process for a few minutes. Slowly add remaining 1/2 cup of lukewarm water while processing until dough is soft and pulls itself away from the sides of the bowl to form a ball. Remove dough and knead on a floured board with hands for a few minutes. If dough is sticky add a little more flour.
Cover dough and allow it to rise for 30 minutes (only)
in a warm place.

Estimated time of preparation: 45 minutes

Meat Pizza
(sfeeHa)

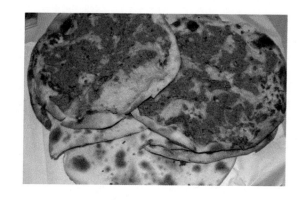

SERVES 6
571 calories per serving

1 recipe	pie dough, prepared (page 11)
1/2 teaspoon	salt (optional)
1/2 teaspoon	cinnamon
1/2 teaspoon	ground allspice
2 tablespoons	butter
3/4 pound	ground lean beef meat
1 large	onion finely chopped
2 large	tomatoes, skin peeled and diced
1/4 cup	pine nuts

Prepare 1 Pie Dough recipe. Add salt, cinnamon and allspice to meat. Sauté meat in butter until light brown (approximately 8 minutes). Add onions and sauté until limp (approximately 6 minutes). Add tomatoes and mix well for 3 minutes under medium fire. Preheat oven to 400°F. Divide dough into 6 equal portions and form into balls. Let rest for 15 minutes. Roll each portion on a floured board to 1/4 inch thickness 6-8 inch diameter depending on the size of the dough balls you made). Fold edges of dough up 1/4 inch to form a rim. Spread meat filling on dough. Sprinkle pine nuts on top. Place on a baking sheet lightly sprayed with vegetable oil. Bake sfeeHa for approximately 15 to 20 minutes or until bottom of pie is golden brown. Broil for 1 to 2 minutes until top is golden. Served with yogurt and salad.

Estimated time of preparation: 75 minutes
Estimated time of baking: 22 minutes

Za'tar Pizza
(mnaqeesh bil za'tar)

SERVES 6 | 517 calories per serving

1 recipe	pie dough, prepared (page 11)
6 tablespoons	Za'tar (thyme)
6 tablespoons	Olive Oil

Prepare 1 Pie Dough recipe. Preheat oven to 450°F. Mix za'tar and oil well. Divide dough into 6 equal portions and form into balls.Llet rest for 15 minutes.   Press each piece with fingers to make a 1/4 inch thick circle (6-8 inch diameter depending on the size of the dough balls you made). Pour 2 tablespoons za'tar/oil mixture on dough and spread over entire top surface of circle. Press fingers on top of circle to leave impressions on the dough. Place circles on a pizza pan sprayed with vegetable oil. Bake until bottom of pie is golden brown.
(approximately 8-10 minutes)

Estimated time of preparation: 50 minutes
Estimated time of cooking: 16 minutes

Spinach Pie
(ftayer bil sbanigh)

SERVES 12 | 335 calories per serving
(2 pieces per serving)

1 recipe	pie dough, prepared (page 11)
1 1/2 pounds	fresh spinach leaves, washed, drained and coarsely chopped*
2 teaspoons	salt (optional)
1	onion finely chopped
1 cup	finely chopped parsley leaves
2 tablespoons	dried & minced mint leaves
1/4 cup	freshly squeezed lemon juice
1 tablespoon	sumac (optional)
1 teaspoon	ground allspice
1/4 teaspoon	hot pepper (optional)
1/4 cup	olive oil

* Canned spinach leaves can also be used. Swiss chard leaves may be substituted.

Prepare 1 Pie Dough recipe. While rising, prepare filling as follows: sprinkle salt on wet spinach leaves. Let sit for 10 minutes until leaves are limp. Take spinach leaves between palms of both hands and squeeze knead until spinach is wilted and water has been drained out. If canned spinach leaves are used, there is no need to salt the leaves. Place spinach in a bowl. Add onions, parsley, mint, lemon juice, sumac, ground allspice, hot pepper and olive oil and mix well. Preheat oven to 400°F. Divide dough into 6 equal portions and, form into balls. Let rest 15 minutes. Roll each portion on a floured board to 1/4 inch thickness (6-8 inch diameter depending on size of balls you made). Cut each rolled piece of dough into 4 equal pieces along its diameter (pieces are near triangular in shape). Place 2 tablespoons of spinach filling in the center of each triangular piece. Fold tips of triangle up to its center and pinch edges of pie well. Place spinach pies on a baking sheet sprayed with vegetable or olive oil and bake for 15 minutes or until bottom of pie is golden brown.

Estimated time of preparation: 70 minutes
Estimated time of baking: 30 minutes

Cheese Pizza
(mnaqeesh bil jibin)

SERVES 6 | 593 calories per serving

1 recipe pie dough, prepared (page 11)
16 ounces shredded Mozzarella cheese

Prepare 1 Pie Dough recipe. Preheat oven to 400°F. Divide dough into 6 equal portions and form balls. Let rest for 15 minutes. Roll each portion into a circle 1/4 inch thick (6-8 inches in diameter depending on the size of dough balls you made). Four ounces of shredded cheese on one half of circle. Fold the other half of circle over the cheese. Crimp edges with fingers or fork. Bake cheese pizza for approximately 15-20 minutes until bottom of pie is golden brown. Broil for 1 minute.

Estimated time of preparation: 55 minutes
Estimated time of baking: 16 minutes

Kishek Pie
(ftayer bil kishek)

SERVES 12 | 358 calories per serving
(2 pieces per serving)

1 recipe	pie dough, prepared (page 11)
1 cup	kishek
1 medium	onion finely chopped
1/2 teaspoon	ground allspice
1/2 teaspoon	salt (optional)
2	tomatoes, chopped
1/2 cup	labni (page 47)
1/4 cup	lukewarm water

Prepare 1 Pie Dough recipe. Place kishek in a bowl. Add onions, allspice, salt, tomatoes, labni and water. Mix well. Preheat oven to 400°F. Divide dough into 6 equal portions, and form into balls. Let dough rest for 15 minutes. Roll each portion on a floured board to 1/4 inch thickness (6-8 inch diameter depending on the size of the balls you made). Cut each rolled piece of dough into 4 equal pieces along its diameter (pieces are near triangular in shape). Place 1 Tablespoon of kishek filling in the center of each triangular piece. Fold tips of triangle to its center and pinch edges of pie well. Place kishek pies on a baking sheet coated with olive oil. Bake pies for 15 minutes or until bottom is golden brown.

Estimated time of preparation: 50 minutes
Estimated time of baking: 30 minutes

Egg Pie
(ftayer bil bayd)

SERVES 6 | 583 calories per serving

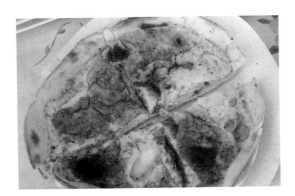

1 recipe	pie dough, prepared (page 11)
10 large	eggs or equivalent egg beaters
1/2 teaspoon	salt (optional)
1/2 teaspoon	ground allspice
1/4 teaspoon	cinnamon

In a mixing bowl beat eggs, salt, allspice and cinnamon.
Preheat oven to 400°F. Split dough into 6 equal portions,
form into a ball. Let rest 15 minutes. Using fingers, press
each portion into a flat circle 1/4 inch thick (6-8 inch diameter
depending on the size of the ball you made). Fold edges
of each circle upward 1/2 inch. Bake dough circles for 5-6
minutes only. Remove from oven. Press dough with fingers
one more time and pour egg mixture into circles to just below
the rim. Place egg pies back in the oven for 15 minutes until
eggs are done. Broil for 30 seconds.

Estimated time of preparation: 1 hour
Estimated time of cooking: 16 minutes

Meat Pie
(ftayer bil laHm, sambusek)

SERVES 40 | 203 calories per serving
(2 pies per serving)

1 recipe kibbi stuffing (page 62)
1 recipe pie dough (no active yeast added), (page 11)
2 cups olive oil (approximately 1 cup will be
consumed after meat pies are fried)

Divide dough into 2 equal portions. Roll each portion on a
floured board to 1/4 inch thickness. Using a circular cookie
cutter (2 inches in diameter) or the rim of glass cup, cut
dough into small circles. Place 1 tsp. of meat stuffing in a line
in the middle of the circle. Moisten edges with water. Fold
the circle in half over stuffing and crimps edges with fingers
or a fork. In a 9 inch skillet fry meat pie until golden brown.
Turn pies over to fry other side until golden brown. Remove
with a slotted spoon and drain on paper towels.

Estimated time of preparation: 90 minutes
Estimated time of cooking: 60 minutes

Meat-Stuffed Fillo Dough
(rqaqat bil laHm)

SERVES 50 | 84 calories per serving
(2 pieces per serving)

    1 recipe kibbi stuffing (page 62)
      1 box fillo dough
      1 cup melted butter

Follow package directions for defrosting fillo dough.
Use 3 sheets for every piece. With a brush, lightly butter
one side of each fillo dough sheet. Place the sheets on top
of each other with buttered side up. Cut dough into four –
4 to 5 inch strips. Place 1 teaspoon of stuffing 1/2 inch from
the top of each strip. Fold opposing edges of fillo over meat
and roll into a cylinder. Place cylinders on a baking sheet
sprayed with vegetable oil. Bake in oven until golden brown
(approximately 20 minutes).

Estimated time of preparation: 1 hour
Estimated time of cooking: 20 minutes

Salads

Tabouli

(tabouli)

SERVES 6 | 409 calories per serving

1/2 cup	medium size crushed wheat (burghul)
5 cups	finely chopped parsley leaves
1 tablespoon	minced dried mint
	or 1/3 cup finely chopped fresh mint
1 medium	onion finely diced
	or 1 cup sliced fresh green onions
2 large	tomatoes finely diced (12 ounces)
1 cup	olive oil
1/3 cup	fresh lemon juice
1 teaspoon	salt (optional)
1/4 teaspoon	ground pepper (optional)

Soak burghul in water for 5 minutes and drain. Place in a large bowl. Add to burghul parsley and mint. Onions, tomatoes, oil, lemon juice and seasonings are added up to 2 hours prior to serving and all ingredients are mixed thoroughly well (keep refrigerated). May be served with Romaine lettuce or cabbage leaves which are used to scoop salad in bite-size servings.

Estimated time of preparation: 20 minutes

Yogurt and Cucumber Salad
(slatet laban bil khyar)

SERVES 6 | 160 calories per serving

1 recipe	basic yogurt (page 46)
	or 32 ounce store bought yogurt
2 cloves	garlic
1 teaspoon	salt (optional)
1/2 teaspoon	dried mint
1 large	cucumber, peeled and sliced in 1/4 inch pieces

Mash garlic with salt. Add garlic, mint and cucumber to
yogurt. Mix well. Refrigerate and serve.

Estimated time of preparation: 6 minutes

Potato Salad

(slatet batata)

SERVES 8 | 209 calories per serving

5 medium	potatoes (approximately 2 pounds)
2 cloves	garlic
1 1/2 teaspoons	salt (optional)
2 teaspoons	mustard
1/2 teaspoon	ground allspice
1/4 cup	fresh lemon juice
1/4 cup	olive oil
4 large	eggs, boiled, shell removed and sliced
1/4 cup	finely chopped parsley leaves or 2 tablespoons dried parsley

In a pan, cover potatoes in water. Add 1 teaspoon salt.
Heat to boil. Cover pan and simmer under medium heat until
tender (approximately 30 minutes). Peel skin and cube into
1 inch pieces. Mash garlic with 1/2 teaspoon salt and add
mustard, pepper, lemon juice and oil to garlic and mix well.
Add garlic/mustard mixture to potatoes and mix well.
Add eggs and parsley on top of potatoes.

Estimated time of preparation: 75 minutes

Green Thyme Salad
(slatet za'tar akhdar)

SERVES 3 | 213 calories per serving

1/2 cup	green thyme leaves*, washed and dried
1/4 cup	fresh lemon juice
2 medium	tomatoes, skin peeled and diced
1 small	onion finely chopped
1/4 cup	olive oil
1/4 teaspoon	salt (optional)

Rosemary can be substituted.

Mix all ingredients. Serve with pita bread. An easy way to remove leaves from thyme stems is to hold the top of the stem and slide fingers down holding firmly.

Estimated time of preparation: 30 minutes

Bread Salad
(fatoush)

SERVES 8 | 306 calories per serving

2 cloves	garlic
1 teaspoon	salt (optional)
3 tablespoons	fresh lemon juice
3/4 cup	olive oil
1 large	cucumber sliced into 1/4 inch slices
2 large	coarsely chopped tomatoes
1 head	romaine lettuce, leaves cut into bite size pieces
1 small	onion finely chopped
1/2 cup	finely chopped parsley leaves
1/2 cup	finely chopped fresh mint leaves (or 1 teaspoon dried minced leaves)
1 cup	snipped purslane leaves (optional)
1 tablespoon	sumac (optional)
2	10 inch diameter Lebanese pita bread baked in oven until light brown and broken into 1 inch pieces

Mash garlic with salt. Add lemon and oil to garlic and mix well. Mix remaining ingredients except bread with garlic/oil mixture. Refrigerate. Prior to serving add bread and mix well.

Estimated time of preparation: 30 minutes

Mixed Vegetables Salad
(slatet mounawa')

SERVES 6 | 135 calories per serving

3 cloves	garlic
1/2 teaspoon	salt (optional)
1/4 cup	fresh lemon juice
1/2 cup	olive oil
1 large	1/4 inch sliced cucumber
2 large	coarsely chopped tomatoes
1 small	head of lettuce, leaves torn
1/4 cup	finely chopped mint leaves (or 1 teaspoon dried minced leaves)
1 cup	snipped purslane leaves (optional)

Mash garlic with salt. Add lemon and oil to garlic and mix well. Mix all above vegetables with garlic/oil mixture. Serve after refrigeration.

Estimated time of preparation: 20 minutes

Swiss Chard Stems with Tahini
(dlou' seliq bil tahini)

SERVES 4 | 213 calories per serving

    1/2 pound   swiss chard stems
       1 recipe   taratour (page 152)

Place Swiss chard stems in boiling water and simmer under medium fire for 5 minutes. Place in a strainer and let cool. In a mixing bowl, place taratour and Swiss chard stems and mix well.

Estimated time of preparation: 20 minutes

Lima Bean Salad
(slatet fasoulia bayda)

SERVES 4 | 426 calories per serving

1 cup	dried lima beans
4 cloves	garlic
1/2 teaspoon	salt (optional)
1/2 cup	olive oil
1/4 cup	lemon juice
1/4 cup	parsley leaves, finely chopped

Soak beans in water for 2 hours. Drain and place beans in a pan and cover with fresh water. Heat to boil. Simmer under medium fire for 30 minutes or until beans are tender. Place in a strainer and let cool. Mash garlic with salt and add oil and lemon and mix well. In a bowl add garlic/oil mixture and lima beans and mix well. Sprinkle parsley on top.

Estimated time of preparation: 45 minutes

Root Beet and Cabbage Salad
(slatet malfouf ma' shmandar)

SERVES 6 | 133 calories per serving

3 large	root beets
4 cloves	garlic
1/2 teaspoon	salt (optional)
1/2 cup	olive oil
1/2 cup	fresh lemon juice
8 ounces	cabbage leaves, shredded

Place root beets in a pan and cover with water. Heat to boil. Simmer under medium fire for approximately 30 minutes or until tender. Place in a strainer and let cool. Peel skin and cube into one inch pieces. Mash garlic with salt. Add oil and lemon to garlic and stir well. In a mixing bowl mix cabbage, root beets and garlic/oil dressing.

Estimated time of preparation: 45 minutes

Green Bean Salad
(lubyet mtabli)

SERVES 4 | 200 calories per serving

2 pounds	green beans, ends snipped and cut into 2 inch pieces
1 teaspoon	salt, divided
4 cloves	garlic
1/4 cup	olive oil
1/4 cup	fresh lemon juice

Place green beans and 1/2 teaspoon salt in a pan. Cover with water. Heat to boil. Simmer under medium heat for approximately 40 minutes or until tender. Place in a strainer and let cool. Mash garlic with 1/2 teaspoon salt. Add oil and lemon juice to garlic and mix well. Place garlic/oil mixture and green beans in a salad bowl and mix well.

Estimated time of preparation: 50 minutes

Potato Salad with Tahini
(batata bil tahini)

SERVES 4 | 402 calories per serving

          5 medium   potatoes
        1 teaspoon   salt (optional)
           1 recipe   taratour (page 152)

Place potatoes in a pan and cover with water. Add salt.
Heat to boil and then simmer under medium fire for
approximately 25 minutes or until tender. Drain and let cool.
Peel skin and cube into 1 inch pieces. Place in a bowl and
pour taratour on top.

Estimated time of preparation: 30 minutes

Flavors of Lebanon |

Soups

Vegetable & Meat Soup
(shurbat laHm ma' khudar)

SERVES 8 | 139 calories per serving

8 cups	water
2/3 pound	cubed lean beef meat chunks
3/4 teaspoon	salt (optional)
1/2 teaspoon	cinnamon
1/4 teaspoon	ground allspice (optional)
2 medium	carrots skin peeled & sliced
1 medium	onion diced
1 small	zucchini sliced
1 large	tomato diced
3/4 cups	green beans cut in 1 inch pieces
1 medium	potato skin peeled and diced
1/3 cup	regular white rice

Place meat and salt in water. Heat to boil. Skim foam from surface of liquid as it accumulates. Add seasonings. Cover and simmer under low to medium heat until meat is tender (approximately 60 minutes). Add vegetables and rice and simmer until tender (approximately 25 minutes). Additional water may be needed to replace evaporated water.

Estimated time of preparation: 15 minutes
Estimated time of cooking: 100 minutes

Vegetable & Chicken Soup
(shurbat djaj ma' khudar)

SERVES 8 | 110 calories per serving

8 cups	water
2/3 pound	cubed boneless chicken breast
3/4 teaspoon	salt (optional)
2 medium	carrots, skin peeled and sliced
1 small	onion diced
1 small	zucchini sliced
3/4 cup	green beans cut into 1 inch pieces
1 medium	potato skin peeled and diced
1/3 cup	white regular rice
1/4 teaspoon	cinnamon
1/8 teaspoon	allspice ground pepper

Place chicken and salt in water. Heat to boil. Skim foam from surface of liquid. Cover and simmer under medium heat until chicken is tender (approximately 30 minutes). When chicken is tender add vegetables, rice and seasonings and cook until vegetables are tender (approximately 25 minutes).

Estimated time of preparation: 15 minutes
Estimated time of cooking: 60 minutes

Rice & Meat Soup
(shurbat mawzat ma' riz)

SERVES 5 | 243 calories per serving

6 cups	water
1 pound	cubed lean beef meat
3/4 teaspoon	salt (optional)
1/2 cup	white regular rice
1/4 cup	chopped parsley leaves
1/4 teaspoon	allspice
1/4 teaspoon	cinnamon

Place meat, cinnamon, allspice and salt in water. Heat to boil. Skim foam from surface of liquid as it accumulates. Cover and simmer under low to medium heat until meat is tender (approximately 60 minutes). Add rice and parsley and simmer until rice is cooked (approximately 20 minutes). Additional water may be needed.

Estimated time of preparation: 15 minutes
Estimated time of cooking: 80 minutes

Rice & Chicken Soup
(shurbat djaj ma' riz)

SERVES 5 | 273 calories per serving

6 cups	water
1 1/2 pounds	cubed boneless chicken breast
1/2 teaspoon	salt (optional)
1/2 cup	white regular rice
1/4 teaspoon	cinnamon
1/4 teaspoon	ground allspice

Place chicken and salt in water. Heat to boil. Skim foam from surface of liquid. Cover and simmer under medium heat until chicken is tender (approximately 30 minutes). When chicken is tender add rice and seasonings and cook until rice is tender (approximately 20 minutes). Additional water may be needed.

Estimated time of preparation: 10 minutes
Estimated time of cooking: 50 minutes

Lentil Soup
(shurbat adas)

SERVES 5 | 404 calories per serving

1 medium	onion finely chopped
1/2 cup	vegetable oil
6 cups	water
1 cup	whole or split lentils washed & drained
1/2 cup	regular white rice washed, soaked in water for 1/2 hour & drained
1/2 teaspoon	salt (optional)

Sauté onions with oil until light brown. In a pan place lentils in water with salt. Heat to boil. Parboil lentils under medium heat (approximately 45 minutes). Add rice and onions/oil mixture to lentils and stir frequently while simmering under medium fire for approximately 20 minutes until both lentils and rice are cooked. Add water as necessary.

Estimated time of preparation: 10 minutes
Estimated time of cooking: 65 minutes

Meat Ball Soup
(shurbat eima)

SERVES 6 | 243 calories per serving

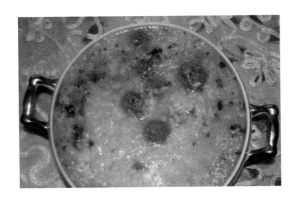

1 pound	ground lean beef meat
1/2 teaspoon	allspice
1/4 teaspoon	cinnamon
1/2 teaspoon	salt (optional)
2 tablespoons	butter
6 cups	water
1/2 cup	regular rice washed and drained
1/4 cup	finely chopped parsley

In a food processor, add meat and seasonings and mix well.
Make meat in 1 inch spheres. Sauté meat with butter until
light brown (approximately 12 minutes). In a pan heat water
to boil.
Add meat and rice and simmer for 25 minutes or until rice is
tender. Add parsley.

Estimated time of preparation: 20 minutes
Estimated time of cooking: 40 minutes

Crushed Wheat & Yogurt Soup
(shurbat kishek)

SERVES 5 | 273 calories per serving

3/4 pound	ground lean beef meat
1 tablespoon	butter
4 cloves	garlic
1/2 teaspoon	salt (optional)
5 cups	water
1 cup	kishek (crushed wheat and yogurt)

In a pan sauté meat in butter until light brown (approximately 8 minutes). Mash garlic with salt. Add garlic to meat and sauté for 2 more minutes. Add water and kishek to meat and stir well. Heat to boil and simmer for approximately 10 minutes.

Estimated time of preparation: 15 minutes
Estimated time of cooking: 20 minutes

Tomato & Onion Soup
(shurbat banadoura ma' basal)

SERVES 4 | 78 calories per serving

1 large	onion thinly sliced
1 tablespoon	butter
4 cups	tomato juice (fresh or canned)
1/2 cup	finely chopped parsley
1/4 teaspoon	allspice ground
1/2 teaspoon	salt (optional)

In a saucepan sauté onion with butter until limp (approximately 6 minutes). Add tomato juice, parsley, pepper and salt. Heat to boil. Simmer under medium fire for 8 minutes.

Estimated time of preparation: 5 minutes
Estimated time of cooking: 15 minutes

Lentils & Swiss Chard Soup
(adas bil Hamoud)

SERVES 8 | 363 calories per serving

7 cups	water
1 1/2 cups	lentils, washed and drained
3 medium	potatoes, skin peeled and cubed
1 pound	swiss chard cut into 1 inch pieces
5 cloves	garlic
1/2 teaspoon	salt (optional)
1 large	onion coarsely chopped
1/2 cup	olive oil
2 teaspoons	dried coriander
1/2 cup	fresh lemon juice

In a pan, heat water to boil. Add lentils and parboil under medium heat for approximately 15 minutes. Add potatoes and swiss chard and simmer for 15 minutes or until vegetables are tender. Meanwhile, mash garlic with salt. Sauté onions with oil until light brown. Add to onions, crushed garlic and coriander and sauté for 2 more minutes. Add garlic/onion mixture and lemon juice to lentils and Swiss chard. Simmer for 15 more minutes or until lentils are done.

Estimated time of preparation: 30 minutes
Estimated time of cooking: 85 minutes

Lentils & Dough Pie Soup
(reshta)

SERVES 6 | 442 calories per serving

1/3 recipe	basic dough (page 10) (no yeast is necessary) or 1 package of frozen homestyle noodles
7 cups	water
1 cup	lentils, washed and drained
1/2 teaspoon	salt (optional)
1 large	onion finely chopped
1/2 cup	olive oil

Prepare 1/3 recipe basic dough. Heat water to boil. Add lentils and salt and simmer for approximately 20 minutes or until lentils are tender. Meanwhile roll dough to 1/8 inch thickness and place on a floured board. Cut dough into long spaghetti-like pieces (1/4 inch thickness). Sauté onions in oil until light brown (approximately 10 minutes). Add onions to lentils and simmer under low heat for approximately 10 minutes. Add dough to lentils and onions and simmer for 10 more minutes. Stir while cooking. Add water as necessary.

Estimated time of preparation: 90 minutes
Estimated time of cooking: 40 minutes

Mixed Grains Soup
(makhlouta)

SERVES 6 | 338 calories per serving

1/4 cup	red beans
1/4 cup	white beans
1/4 cup	garbanzo beans
10 cups	water
1/4 cup	lentils
1 large	onion finely chopped
1/2 cup	olive oil
5 whole	cloves garlic
1/4 cup	white regular rice
1/4 cup	coarse burghul
1 teaspoon	salt (optional)

Soak beans (red, white and garbanzo) overnight. Wash beans
and drain. In a pan heat 10 cups water to boil. Add beans
and parboil for approximately 30 minutes. Add Lentils to
beans and parboil for 20 minutes. Meanwhile Sauté onion
with oil until light brown (for approximately 10 minutes).
Add onion, garlic cloves, rice and burghul and simmer for
20 more minutes. Stir frequently while cooking.

Estimated time of preparation: 10 minutes
Estimated time of cooking: 100 minutes

Yogurt Dishes

Basic Yogurt
(laban)

SERVES 8 | 113 calories per serving

    1/2 gallon 2% or whole milk
2 tablespoons plain yogurt from previously prepared
                     or commercially purchased yogurt

Place milk in a heavy pan and heat under low fire. When milk comes to just a boil (just under 212 ° remove from fire and let it warm down until you are able to immerse your finger in the milk to the count of 10. In a small container mix plain yogurt (also called rawbi or starter milk) with 1/4 cup of the warm milk from the pan together. Add this mixture to the warm milk in the pan and stir. Cover with a lid and place towels or a blanket over pan to keep warm. Keep pan in a warm place and do not disturb for 12 hours. Cool yogurt in the refrigerator for 4 hours prior to serving.

Estimated time of preparation: 20 minutes

Yogurt Spread
(labni)

SERVES 13 | 70 calories per serving

1 recipe   basic yogurt (page 46)
             or 64 ounces of store bought plain yogurt
2 tablespoons   salt (optional)

Place cold yogurt in a strainer covered with one layer
of cheese cloth or 2 layers of kitchen paper towel. Let
yogurt drains in a container placed in the refrigerator for
approximately 6 to 8 hours. Remove labni from strainer.
Add salt and mix well. Keep refrigerated in a covered
container. Labni is usually spread on bread with a sprinkle
of olive oil and olives.

Labni Preserved Balls
(labni mkadsi)

SERVES 13 | 147 calories per serving

1 recipe	yogurt spread (page 47)
	or 64 ounces of store bought plain yogurt
2 tablespoons	salt
3 cups	Vegetable oil
2 – 16 ounce	canning jars with lids, sterilized

Labni should be refrigerated in a strainer overnight. Add salt
to labni and mix well. Make labni in 1 inch spheres using
the palms of both hands. Pour little oil on both hands to
facilitate making the spheres. Place spheres on paper towels
for 2-3 hours to dry well. Place dried spheres in a sterile jar.
Cover with oil and seal jar well. Store in refrigerator for
up to 1 week. Labni spheres are spread on pita bread along
with olive oil.

Estimated time of preparation: 25 minutes

Yogurt & Garbanzo Beans
(fatte´ bil laban)

SERVES 5 | 501 calories per serving

1 1/2 cups	dried chickpeas or 3 cups canned chickpeas
1/2 teaspoon	baking soda (omit if using canned chick peas)
1 cup	garbanzo bean water
	(saved from boiling beans or can)
1/4 cup	pine nuts
1/2 tablespoon	butter
4 cloves	garlic
1/2 teaspoon	salt (optional)
3 cups	basic yogurt (page 46)
	or 3 cups of store bought plain yogurt
2 loaves	Arabic bread, toasted and broken into
	1 inch pieces
2 tablespoons	melted butter
1/4 teaspoon	allspice

Soak dried garbanzo beans in water with 1/2 teaspoon baking soda for 1 hour. Wash well with water, drain and place in a pan. Cover with water. Heat to boil. Simmer under medium fire for approximately 90 minutes or until tender. Drain garbanzo water after saving 1 cup. If canned garbanzo beans are used skip above step. Save 1 cup of water from the can. Sauté pine seeds with 1/2 tablespoon butter until light brown (approximately 5 minutes). In a bowl, mash garlic with salt. Add yogurt to garlic and mix well. In a salad bowl, place bread. On top of bread place garbanzo beans, saved garbanzo water, yogurt, pine nuts, then pour melted butter on top of yogurt. Sprinkle pepper over yogurt. Do not mix. Fatte´ could be served as breakfast or lunch. It is best served immediately after preparation.

Estimated time of preparation: 15 minutes
Estimated time of cooking (if dried beans used): 95 minutes

Stuffed Zucchini & Yogurt
(kousa MeHshi bil laban)

SERVES 8 | 423 calories per serving

14 small	zucchini, 5-6 inches in length (approximately 5 pound)
1 pound	ground lean beef meat
3 tablespoons	butter
1/2 teaspoon	ground allspice
1/2 teaspoon	cinnamon
1-1/2 teaspoons	salt (optional)
1 cup	regular white rice
2 cups	water
1 recipe	basic yogurt (page 46) or 64 ounces of store bought plain yogurt
1 tablespoon	corn starch
1	egg white or equivalent egg beaters
1/2 teaspoon	dried and minced mint leaves
5 cloves	garlic

Slice the growth end of each zucchini. Core zucchini using the end of a small teaspoon or a zucchini corer leaving a 1/4 inch thick wall. Do not pierce through zucchini wall. Wash zucchini after coring and let drain in a strainer. Sauté beef meat in butter until light brown. Add seasonings, salt and rice. Mix well and sauté further for 5 more minutes. Fill 3/4 of zucchini core with filling. Place stuffed zucchini in a large pan. Boil 2 cups of water and pour over zucchini. Cover pan and simmer for 10 minutes. In a separate pan place yogurt, corn starch, whole egg and mix well. After heating yogurt to boil, stir well with a whisk. Add yogurt, garlic and mint to zucchini. Mash garlic with 1/2 teaspoon salt and add to yogurt. Simmer under medium heat until zucchini tender (approximately 25 minutes). Do not cover pan while simmering zucchini.

Estimated time of preparation: 90 minutes
Estimated time of cooking: 55 minutes

Kibbi with Yogurt
(labnieh)

SERVES 8 | 437 calories per serving

1/2 recipe	kibbi (page 61)
2-3 cups	vegetable oil for frying
1/2 cup	regular white rice
2 cups	water
1 recipe	basic yogurt (page 46)
	or 64 ounces of store bought plain yogurt
1	egg white or equivalent egg beaters
1 tablespoon	corn starch
1 teaspoon	salt

Make kibbi in hollow spheres of 2 inches diameter. Heat oil
in pan and fry kibbee spheres for 3-5 minutes until reddish
hue is seen. Remove from heat and drain on paper towel.
When cool enough to handle pierce small holes in every
sphere with a fork. Place rice in a pan. Add 2 cups water.
Parboil rice under medium heat for approximately 10 minutes.
Meanwhile place yogurt in a separate pan. Add egg white
and cornstarch and heat to just a boil. While heating yogurt
stir continuously with a whisk. Add rice, kibbi and salt to
yogurt. Simmer for approximately 10 minutes stirring often.
Can serve either warm or after refrigeration.

Estimated time of preparation: 25 minutes
Estimated time of cooking: 35 minutes

Beef with Yogurt
(laban immu)

SERVES 5 | 445 calories per serving

1 pound	cubed lean beef meat
1 teaspoon	salt (optional)
5 cups	water
1 pound	small whole onions (1 inch), skin peeled
1 recipe	basic yogurt (page 46)
	or 64 ounces of store bought plain yogurt
1 tablespoon	corn starch
1	egg white or equivalent egg beaters

Prepare 1 basic yogurt recipe (commercial plain yogurt can be used). Place meat and salt in a pan. Add 5 cups of water to meat. Heat to boil. Simmer under medium heat for approximately 30 minutes. Skim foam from surface of liquid as it accumulates. Add peeled whole onions to meat and cook until onions are limp. In a separate pan place yogurt, beaten egg and corn starch. Heat to boil. While heating stir continuously with a whisk. Place yogurt on top of meat and onions and mix well. Simmer under medium heat for 10 more minutes or until meat is tender. Serve with rice pilaf.

Estimated time of preparation: 10 minutes
Estimated time of cooking: 65 minutes

Meat Stuffed Pastries with Yogurt
(shishbarak)

SERVES 12 | 490 calories per serving
(6-7 dumplings per serving)

Dumplings consists of dough and meat filling.

You may choose to buy frozen dumplings such as tortellini at the store. If so, please skip down to yogurt Sauce preparation. Add the dumplings directly into the sauce and heat through for 20 minutes or until dumplings are cooked through.

For the dough:

3 cups	all-purpose white flour
1/2 teaspoon	salt (optional)
1/2 cup	olive oil
1 cup	water

For the meat filling:

1 pound	ground lean beef meat
2 tablespoons	butter
1 large	onion finely chopped
1/2 teaspoon	ground allspice
1/2 teaspoon	cinnamon

Continued next page.

For the yogurt sauce:

1 recipe	basic yogurt (page 46)
	or 64 ounces of store bought plain yogurt
1	egg white or equivalent egg beaters
2 tablespoon	corn starch
1 teaspoon	salt
1 cup	water or more as needed to reach creamy consistency
2 Tablespoons	butter
8 cloves	garlic
1 bunch	green coriander or 1 teaspoon dried coriander
2 Tablespoons	dried mint (optional)
1 cup	pine nuts (optional)
	sautéed in 2 tablespoons of butter

For the rice pilaf (double recipe - page 109)

For the dough:
In a food processor place flour, salt, olive oil, and water. Process until dough pulls away from the sides of the bowl. Add small increments of lour as needed until a soft dough is formed. Let dough rest for 1 hour.

For the meat filling:
Sauté meat in 2 tbsp. butter until brown (approximately 10 minutes). Add onions, allspice and cinnamon to meat and sauté for 10 more minutes.

To prepare the dumpling:
Preheat oven to 350°F. Using a rolling pin, roll dough out to 1/4 inch thickness. Using a 2 inch biscuit cutter, cut dough into round circles. Place 1 teaspoon of stuffing in center of every small circle. Fold the circle in half and seal well. You can stop here at the half moon or you can go even further by taking the edges of the half moon around to the back, folding one edge over the other, and sealing well with a pinch. Place meat-filled pastries on greased cookie sheet or baking pan. Bake for approximately 25 minutes or until dough dries and turns golden brown.

Flavors of Lebanon

To prepare yogurt sauce:
In a pan place yogurt and heat to boiling. Once a boil is reached, add. egg white, cornstarch, salt, and water. Reduce heat to low. You want to reach a creamy smooth consistency. While heating stir yogurt often with a whisk. In a separate pan sautee cilantro and garlic in butter for 5 minutes. Add this to yogurt and continue to stir constantly for 5 minutes.

Assemble the dish:
Place 1/2 cup rice pilaf in bowl, followed by 6-7 baked dumplings. Pour a ladle of yogurt sauce over rice and dumplings. Garnish with mint and pine nuts if desired.

Estimated time of preparation: 90 minutes
Estimated time of cooking: 50 minutes

Meat Dishes

Lebanese Hamburger
(kafta)

SERVES 4 | 230 calories per serving

1 pound	ground beef meat
1 medium	onion finely chopped
3/4 cup	chopped parsley leaves (1 bunch of parsley)
1/4 teaspoon	cinnamon
1/2 teaspoon	salt (optional)
1/4 teaspoon	ground allspice

Place meat, onions, parsley and seasonings in food processor and mix well. If necessary can add up to 1/4 cup of water to facilitate mixing. Shape either into cylindrical forms around a skewer (will need approximately 12 skewers) or round patties (approximately 8). Barbecue until cooked.

Estimated time of preparation: 10 minutes
Estimated time of cooking: 20 minutes

Baked Kafta & Potatoes
(kafta ma' batata)

SERVES 6 | 422 calories per serving

2 pounds	ground lean beef meat
1 large	onion chopped
1 cup	chopped parsley leaves
1/2 teaspoon	cinnamon
1 teaspoon	salt (optional)
1/2 teaspoon	ground allspice
1 1/2 pounds	potatoes, peeled and thinly (1/4 inch) sliced
3 large	red tomatoes sliced
1 cup	tomato sauce

Preheat oven to 400°F. Place meat, onions, parsley and seasonings in food processor and mix well. If necessary, add up to 1/2 cup of water to facilitate mixing. Spread kafta mix in a 9 x 13 inch baking pan. Place sliced potatoes evenly on top of kafta followed by a layer of sliced tomatoes. Pour tomato sauce on top of meat and vegetables. Cover with aluminum foil and bake in the oven for approximately 60 minutes until meat and vegetables are baked through. You may need to add additional water or tomato sauce if kafta becomes too dry and vegetables are not baking.

Estimated time of preparation: 15 minutes
Estimated time of cooking: 70 minutes

Raw Kibbi
(kibbi nayi)*

SERVES 8 | 366 calories per serving

1 large	onion chopped
1 1/2 pounds	ground lean beef meat
1 teaspoon	dried minced mint leaves
2 1/2 cups	medium size burghul soaked in water for 5 minutes and well drained
1 teaspoon	salt (optional)
1/2 teaspoon	ground allspice

Note: Raw kibbi is very popular in Lebanon. However, we advise cooked kibbi as an alternative to prevent potential food poisoning.

Place onions in a food processor and process finely. Add meat to onions and process for 1 or 2 more minutes. Water may be slowly added as necessary to facilitate mixing (approximately 1/2 cup). Place mixture in a large mixing bowl and add to it mint, burghul and seasonings. Knead mixture thoroughly with hands which should be kept wet by dipping them frequently into cold ice water. Kibbi nayi is served with Arabic bread and a sprinkle of olive oil added to it.

Estimated time of preparation: 30 minutes

Baked Kibbi
(kibbi)

SERVES 8
620 calories per serving

1 large	onion chopped
1 1/2 pounds	ground lean beef meat
1 teaspoon	dried minced mint leaves
3 cups	medium size burghul soaked in water for 5 minutes and well drained
1/2 teaspoon	ground allspice
1/4 teaspoon	cinnamon
3 tablespoons	butter
1 tablespoon	salt (optional)
1 recipe	Kibbi Stuffing (page 62)

Baked kibbi can also be formed in hollow spheres or spheres stuffed with Kibbi Stuffing. To make kibbi spheres, press a hole with forefinger into a 1-inch sphere-sized chunk of kibbi. Expand the hole by pressing shell between forefinger and palm of hand. Sphere is then stuffed if desired and edges are closed. Fry in vegetable oil for a few minutes until they become light brown or bake at 350 degrees for 20 minutes or until baked through.

Prepare kibbi with the addition of cinnamon to recipe. Split kibbi dough into 2 halves. If stuffed kibbi is planned, spread the first half evenly in a 12 inch pan greased with 1 tablespoon oil. Spread the stuffing evenly over kibbi. On a wax paper press second half of kibbi dough with fingers to form a circle (approximately 12 inches in diameter). Use this to facilitate placing the 2nd layer of kibbi. Flip kibbi layer over top of stuffing while matching edges. Remove wax paper and using fingers even out edges and surface of kibbi. Stuffed dough is then cut (full thickness) into 8 pie-shaped pieces. Using forefinger a hole is made in the center of dough. Place butter over kibbi and cook in preheated oven at 400°F for approximately 30 minutes or until baked through. Broil for 2-3 minutes. Serve with salads and pickles.

Estimated time of preparation: 50 minutes
Estimated time of cooking: 55 minutes

Kibbi Stuffing
(Hashwit al kibbi)

SERVES 8 | 176 calories per serving
(stuffing for 1 basic kibbi recipe)

1/2 cup	pine nuts
3 tablespoons	butter, divided
3/4 pound	ground lean beef meat
1 large	onion finely chopped
1/4 teaspoon	cinnamon
1/4 teaspoon	ground allspice
2 teaspoons	salt (optional)
2 teaspoons	sour pomegranate juice (optional)

Sauté pine nuts in 1 tablespoon of butter until golden.
Separately, sauté meat in 2 tablespoons of butter until brown
(approximately 8 minutes). Add onions and seasonings
to meat and sauté until onions are limp (approximately 6
minutes). Add pine nuts and pomegranate to meat and mix
well. Use stuffing when warm (not hot).

Estimated time of preparation: 10 minutes
Estimated time of cooking: 18 minutes

Kibbi & Kishek
(kibbet al kishek)

SERVES 8 | 383 calories per serving

1 large	onion, thinly sliced
1 tablespoon	butter or vegetable oil
4 cloves	garlic, mashed
1 bunch	green coriander, finely chopped
5 cups	water
1 cups	kishek
1 recipe	Baked Kibbi made in hollow spheres (page 61 - see italics)

In a pan, sauté onion in your choice of fat until limp. Add mashed garlic and chopped coriander to onion and sauté for 2 to 3 additional minutes. Add 5 cups of water and kishek to onions, garlic and coriander. Heat to boil. Once boiling, add kibbi spheres (use tooth pick to create 3 holes in each sphere before placing it in boiling water). Simmer under medium heat for 15 minutes.

Estimated time of preparation: 10 minutes
Estimated time of cooking: 75 minutes

Green Bean Meat Stew
(lubieh bil laHm)

SERVES 6 | 199 calories per serving

1 pound	beef chuck, cubed
3 tablespoons	butter
1 large	onion finely chopped
5 cups	water
1 pound	green beans soaked in boiling water, washed, drained, ends sniped and cut into 2 inch pieces
1 large	tomato diced or (1) 15 ounce can diced tomatoes
1 teaspoon	salt (optional)
1/2 teaspoon	ground allspice
1/4 teaspoon	cinnamon

In a pan sauté meat in butter until browned. Add allspice, cinnamon, and salt. Add onions and sauté for 5 more minutes or until limp. Cover with water. Heat to boil. Cover pan and simmer under low to medium heat for approximately 30 minutes or until tender. Add beans, tomato and seasonings, mix well and simmer under medium fire for approximately 30 more minutes until meat and green beans are tender. Warm water might be added as necessary to replace evaporated water. Serve with rice pilaf.

Estimated time of preparation: 10 minutes
Estimated time of cooking: 2 hours

Okra Meat Stew
(bami bil laHm)

SERVES 6 | 498 calories per serving

1 pound	beef chuck, cubed
2 tablespoons	butter
4 cups	water
1/2 teaspoon	cinnamon
2 pounds	fresh young okra or 4 ounces of dried young okra soaked in boiling water for 30 minutes
3/4 cup	vegetable oil
1 teaspoon	salt (optional)
1/4 teaspoon	ground allspice
6 cloves	crushed garlic
1 teaspoon	dried coriander or 1 stalk of chopped green coriander leaves
1/4 cup	sour pomegranate juice (optional)

Sauté meat in butter for approximately 10 minutes or until meat is brown. Cover meat with 4 cups water. Add cinnamon. Heat to boil. Cover pan and simmer under medium heat for approximately 35 minutes. Meanwhile, in a separate pan, fry okra in oil for 5 to 7 minutes or until light brown. Add to okra salt, allspice, coriander, garlic and mix well. Add seasoned okra and pomegranate juice to meat and simmer under medium fire for approximately 30 more minutes or until meat and okra are tender. While cooking warm water might be added as necessary to replace evaporated water. Serve with rice pilaf.

Estimated time of preparation: 20 minutes
Estimated time of cooking: 80 minutes

Sweat Peas Meat Stew
(bazela bil laHm)

SERVES 6 | 264 calories per serving

1 pound	ground beef
2 tablespoons	butter
1 large	onion finely chopped
3 cups	water
8 ounce	can tomato sauce
1/2 teaspoon	allspice ground pepper
1/4 teaspoon	cinnamon
1/2 teaspoon	salt
1 package	frozen peas
5	carrots, peeled and sliced

In a pan sauté meat with butter until browned (approximately 8 minutes). Add onion to meat and sauté until onion is limp. Add water, tomato sauce and seasonings. Heat to boil. Simmer under medium heat for approximately 50 minutes or until meat is tender. Add sweet peas and carrots, and simmer for 5 more minutes. Serve with rice pilaf.

Estimated time of preparation: 10 minutes
Estimated time of cooking: 75 minutes

Flavors of Lebanon |

Stuffed Grape Leaves
(waraq einab)

SERVES 6
336 calories per serving

3/4 pound	ground lean beef meat
2 pounds	beef ribs (optional) to layer between grape leaves
1 teaspoon	salt, divided (optional)
1/2 teaspoon	ground allspice
1/4 teaspoon	cinnamon
2 tablespoons	butter
1 cup	white regular rice, rinsed and drained
50	fresh or canned grape leaves
1 cup	fresh lemon juice

Add allspice, 1/2 teaspoon salt and cinnamon to meat. Sauté meat in butter under medium heat until light brown (approximately 8 minutes). Add rice to meat and mix well. Place leaf with rough edge up. Place 1 tsp. of meat and rice in a row along the lower 1/3 of the leaf. Fold the bottom of leaf over meat/rice mixture, then fold both edges inward and roll the leaf firmly into a cylinder shape. As you roll upward you may need to push edges of leaf in to form an even and smooth edge. The smooth surface of the leaf will be to the outside. In a pan place a few single unstuffed leaves on the bottom of the pan and then place stuffed grape leaves in alternating layers starting from the outer rim of the pan. If you chose to, you can alternate layers of beef ribs with the leaves. Use 3 to 4 individual ribs per layer. Cover the grape leaves with a glass plate to prevent the leaves from floating and unfolding while cooking. Add 1/2 teaspoon salt and just enough water to cover top layer of leaves. Heat to boil. Simmer for 60 minutes or until tender. Add warm water as necessary to replace what has evaporated. When tender and water has almost been evaporated add lemon juice. Serve warm with yogurt and green onions.

Estimated time of preparation: 120 minutes
Estimated time of cooking: 70 minutes

Meat Dishes

White Bean Meat Stew
(fasulya bayda bil laHm)

SERVES 6 | 419 calories per serving

2 cups	white beans, such as great northern
1 pound	chuck beef, cubed
2 tablespoons	butter
1 large	onion finely chopped
5 cups	warm water
1 teaspoon	salt (optional)
1/4 teaspoon	cinnamon
1/2 teaspoon	allspice
8 ounce	can tomato sauce

Soak beans in water overnight. Drain water. In a pan, sauté meat with butter until light brown (approximately 8 minutes). Add onion to meat and sauté for 5 more minutes or until onion is limp. Add water and seasonings. Heat to boil. Simmer under medium heat for approximately 60 minutes. Add tomato sauce and beans, and simmer for 30 more minutes or until beans are tender. Add water as necessary. Serve with rice pilaf.

Estimated time of preparation: 10 minutes
Estimated time of cooking: 105 minutes

Meat Rolls with Eggs
(filet bil bayd)

SERVES 7 | 597 calories per serving

2 pounds	ground lean beef meat
6 large	boiled eggs, shells removed*
1 teaspoon	salt (optional)
1/2 teaspoon	ground allspice
1/2 teaspoon	cinnamon
3/4 cup	butter
4 cups	water
1 tablespoon	flour
1/4 cup	lemon juice
1/4 cup	vinegar
1/4 cup	white wine
1 tablespoon	butter
1 large	can of cooked peas and carrots

pine nuts and garlic cloves can be substituted

Process meat, salt, allspice and cinnamon in food processor. A small amount of water can be added to facilitate processing. Separate meat into three equal portions. Each portion is kneaded on a large plate to 1/4 inch thickness. Place 2 full boiled eggs on each meat portion. Fold in the edges of meat dough and roll it in a cylinder shape with eggs in the middle. A thread is tied around each meat cylinder from end to end in a spiral form to secure meat from unfolding during cooking. In a pan, sauté meat rolls with butter under light fire until brown. Remove to a clean pan and cover with 4 cups of water. Heat to boil. Simmer meat under light fire for 20 minutes or until meat is tender. Remove meat with a slotted strainer and place on a plate in the refrigerator for 1 hour. To the meat broth add flour, lemon juice, vinegar, wine and butter and mix well with a whisk to form a white sauce. Boil for 5 minutes while stirring continuously. The thread over the meat roll is then removed and meat is sliced in 1/2 inch slices. Place meat in a pan and place peas and carrots around it. Heat prior to serving. The sauce is served on the side.

Estimated time of preparation: 60 minutes

Estimated time of cooking: 75 minutes

Burghul with Meat
(burghul mfalfal ma' laHm)

SERVES 7 | 382 calories per serving

1/2 teaspoon	baking soda
1/2 cup	dried garbanzo beans or 1 can drained and rinsed
1 pound	beef chuck, cubed
1/2 teaspoon	salt (optional)
7 cups	water or beef or chicken broth
1 large	coarsely chopped onion
1/2 teaspoon	ground allspice
1/2 teaspoon	cinnamon
2 cups	medium or coarse burghul
2 tablespoons	butter

Omit this step if using canned garbanzo beans. Cover garbanzo beans with water. Add baking soda and soak for 1 hour. Wash garbanzo beans under running water and drain. In a pan, place meat, salt and 7 cups of water. Cover and parboil under medium heat for 30 minutes. Skim foam from surface of liquid as it accumulates. Just before meat is tender, add garbanzo beans, onions, pepper and cinnamon. Cover and simmer under medium heat until garbanzo beans and meat are tender (approximately 60 minutes). Add burghul, cover and simmer under low to medium heat for 15 minutes or until water evaporates. Melt butter in a cup, add on top of cooked burghul and mix. Serve with yogurt.

Estimated time of preparation: 60 minutes
Estimated time of cooking: 120 minutes

Flavors of Lebanon |

Fried Meat with Bread Crumbs
(laHm bil bayd ma' ka'k)

SERVES 6 | 498 calories per serving

2 pounds	ground beef
1 teaspoon	salt (optional)
1/2 teaspoon	allspice
1/2 teaspoon	cinnamon
2 large	eggs beaten or equivalent egg beaters
1 cup	bread crumbs
1/4 cup	vegetable oil
1/4 cup	fresh lemon juice (optional)

Process meat, salt, allspice and cinnamon in food processor.
A small amount of water can be added to facilitate processing.
Separate meat into 4 equal portions. Each portion is kneaded
on a large plate to 1/4 inch thickness. Meat is dipped into
eggs then bread crumbs. Fry meat in vegetable oil until tender
(approximately 12 minutes). Meat pieces are then placed on
a plate and served with Arabic bread. Pour lemon juice on
meat as desired.

Estimated time of preparation: 10 minutes
Estimated time of cooking: 12 minutes

Stuffed Eggplant & Zucchini
(kousa wa batinjan meHshi)

SERVES 7 | 444 calories per serving

1 pound	ground lean beef meat
4 tablespoons	butter, divided
1 cup	white regular rice
1 teaspoon	ground allspice
1/2 teaspoon	cinnamon
1 teaspoon	salt (optional)
2 pounds	zucchini, 6 inches long (approximately 6)
2 pounds	eggplant, 6 inches long (approximately 6)
1 large	onion finely chopped
4 large	tomatoes, skin peeled and finely chopped
3 cups	water
15 ounce	can tomato sauce

Sauté meat with 2 tablespoons butter until brown (approximately 10 minutes). Add to meat the rice, salt, allspice and cinnamon. Mix well. Sauté for 4 more minutes. Core zucchini and eggplants using the end of a small teaspoon or a zucchini corer leaving a 1/4 inch thick wall. Do not pierce through zucchini or eggplant wall. Wash after coring and let drain in a strainer. Stuff 3/4 of each zucchini and eggplant with meat and rice filling. In a large pan, sauté onions with 2 tablespoons butter until limp. Add tomatoes and sauce, and sauté for 5 more minutes. Add to onions and tomatoes the 3 cups of water. Heat to boil. Once boiled, add eggplant and let simmer for 15 minutes, then add zucchini. Continue simmering for approximately 40 minutes or until zucchini and eggplants are tender. Add warm water as necessary to replace evaporated water.

Estimated time of preparation: 100 minutes
Estimated time of cooking: 85 minutes

Beef Tenderloin & Vegetables
(rosto)

SERVES 10 | 531 calories per serving

4 pounds	whole beef tenderloin
10 cloves	garlic (each split in half)
1/2 cup	butter, divided
1 teaspoon	salt (optional)
1 teaspoon	ground allspice
1 teaspoon	cinnamon
2 tablespoons	flour
1/4 cup	white wine
1/4 cup	vinegar
1 pound	carrots sliced
2 cups	green peas
3 medium	potatoes, cubed and baked

With a knife make 20 slits throughout beef meat (1 inch wide and 1 and 1/2 inches deep). Fill each mini pocket created with 1/2 clove of garlic. Tie a thread around meat to prevent slits from opening during cooking. Sauté meat in 1/2 stick butter under light heat until brown. Place in a large pan. Add salt, allspice and cinnamon. Cover with water. Heat to boil. Simmer under medium heat until tender (90 to 120 minutes). Remove from water and let cool at room temperature , then in the refrigerator. Save meat broth. Allow meat to cool for 2 hours before slicing it into 1/2 inch thick slices. In a pan sauté flour in 2 tablespoons butter for 5 minutes. Add meat broth gradually to flour while stirring with a whisk under medium heat until a thick white sauce is formed. Remove white sauce from heat and add to it wine and vinegar and mix well. Boil carrots and peas in water until tender. Drain water. Add baked potatoes to carrots and peas and sauté in 2 tablespoons butter under medium heat for 5 minutes. Prior to serving warm vegetables and meat.

Estimated time of preparation: 20 minutes
Estimated time of cooking: 3 hours

Meat & Vegetable Dish
(aleb khudra)

SERVES 6 | 280 calories per serving

1 pound	chuck beef, cubed
1/4 cup	butter
1 large	onion, sliced
3 cups	water
3 large	carrots, sliced
1	regular size eggplant, sliced
1	regular size zucchini, sliced
2 cups	fresh green beans, cut into bite size pieces or 1 can may be substituted
3 medium	potatoes, cubed
2 large	tomatoes, chopped
1/2 teaspoon	ground allspice
1 teaspoon	salt (optional)
1/2 teaspoon	cinnamon

In a pan, brown meat in butter until brown. Add onions
and sauté until limp. Add 3 cups of water. Heat to boil.
Cover and simmer under medium heat until meat is tender
(approximately 50 minutes). On top of meat, place vegetables
in layers starting with carrots, zucchini, eggplants, beans,
potatoes and tomatoes. Add remaining seasonings and salt.
Simmer until vegetables are tender (additional 30 minutes).

Estimated time of preparation: 15 minutes
Estimated time of cooking: 85 minutes

Flavors of Lebanon

Meat Balls & Rice
(dawoud basha)

SERVES 6 | 448 calories per serving

2 pounds	ground lean beef meat
1 teaspoon	salt (optional)
1/2 teaspoon	ground allspice
1/2 teaspoon	cinnamon
4 tablespoons	butter, divided
2 large	onions, chopped
1/3 cup	pine nuts
8 ounce	can tomato sauce
3 cups	water

Mix meat, salt, allspice and seasonings well. Mold meat into 1 inch spheres. Sauté spheres in 2 tablespoon butter until brown. Also sauté onion in 1 tablespoon butter until limp. Then sauté pine nuts in 1 tablespoon butter until golden brown. Place meat spheres, onions, pine nuts and tomato sauce in a pan. Add 3 cups water. Heat to boil. Simmer for approximately 30 minutes or until a thick sauce is formed. Serve with rice pilaf.

Estimated time of preparation: 15 minutes
Estimated time of cooking: 60 minutes

Artichokes & Meat
(ardishawkee bil laHm)

SERVES 8
190 calories per serving

1/2 pound	ground lean beef meat
3 tablespoons	butter, divided
1/2 teaspoon	salt (optional)
1/4 teaspoon	ground allspice
1/4 teaspoon	cinnamon
1 large	onion, finely chopped
1/4 cup	pine nuts
1 tablespoon	tomato paste
1 1/2 cups	warm water
8	artichokes, leaves removed, skin peeled and center cored
2 large	tomatoes, sliced into 8 slices

Sauté beef meat with 2 tablespoons butter until brown
(10 minutes). Add allspice, cinnamon, salt and onion. Sauté
further until onion is limp (5 or 6 minutes). In a separate pan,
sauté pine nuts with 1 tablespoon butter. Add pine nuts to
meat and onion and mix well. Mix tomato paste with 1 and
1/2 cups of warm water. Place artichokes in a baking pan.
Fill center of artichokes with meat filling. Pour tomato juice
in the pan . Place one slice of fresh tomato on top of each
stuffed artichokes. Bake in oven preheated to 350°F for
approximately 30 minutes. Serve with rice pilaf.

Estimated time of preparation: 15 minutes
Estimated time of cooking: 50 minutes

Spinach Meat Stew
(sbanigh bil laHm)

SERVES 6 | 307 calories per serving

1 pound	ground lean beef meat
3 tablespoons	butter, divided
1 large	onion, finely chopped
1/4 cup	pine nuts
2 pounds	spinach, washed, drained and torn into 2-3 inch pieces
1 teaspoon	salt (optional)
1/2 teaspoon	ground allspice
1/4 teaspoon	cinnamon
1/2 cup	water
1	fresh lemon (optional)

In a pan. sauté meat with 2 tablespoons butter until brown (8 minutes). Add onions and sauté until limp (7 minutes). Remove from heat. Sauté pine nuts in 1 tablespoon butter until golden. Add pine nuts to meat and onions and mix well. Add to meat, spinach, salt, allspice and cinnamon and 1/2 cup of water. Cover and simmer under low heat for 15 to 20 minutes. Add a squeeze of lemon if desired to each serving. Serve with rice pilaf.

Estimated time of preparation: 5 minutes
Estimated time of cooking: 30 minutes

Rice & Meat Dish
(riz bil laHm)

SERVES 4
520 calories per serving

1 pound	ground beef meat
5 tablespoons	butter, divided
1/4 cup	pine nuts
1 teaspoon	salt (optional)
1-1/2 cups	white regular rice
1/2 teaspoon	ground allspice
1/4 teaspoon	cinnamon
3 cups	water

In a pan, sauté meat in 4 tablespoons butter until brown
(8 minutes). Separately, sauté pine nuts in 1 tablespoon
butter until golden. Add pine nuts, salt, rice, allspice and
cinnamon to meat and mix well under medium heat for
2-3 minutes. Add water to rice and meat and heat to boil.
Once boiling, cover pan and simmer under medium heat
for 15 to 20 minutes.

Estimated time of preparation: 5 minutes
Estimated time of cooking: 35 minutes

Green Fava Bean Meat Stew
(foul akhdar bil laHm)

SERVES 5 | 379 calories per serving

1/2 pound	lean beef meat cut into 1 inch pieces
2 tablespoons	butter
4 cups	water
1 teaspoon	salt (optional)
2 large	onions, chopped
1/2 teaspoon	ground allspice
1/4 teaspoon	cinnamon
1 pound	fresh green fava bean seeds
1 cup	white regular rice

Sauté meat in butter until brown (approximately 8 minutes).
In a pan place meat and water. Heat to boil. Remove
foam from surface of liquid. Cover and parboil meat under
medium heat for 25 minutes. Add salt, onion, allspice and
cinnamon. Simmer for 25 minutes. Add green fava beans
and simmer for 25 more minutes. Then add rice and simmer
for 20 more minutes.

Estimated time of preparation: 10 minutes
Estimated time of cooking: 90 minutes

Meat-Stuffed Eggplants
(sheikh al meHshi)

SERVES 5 | 496 calories per serving

10 small	eggplants, ends snipped
1 cup	olive oil (1/2 cup is consumed)
1/2 pound	ground lean beef meat
1/2 teaspoon	ground allspice
1/2 teaspoon	cinnamon
1/2 teaspoon	salt (optional)
3 tablespoons	butter, divided
1 medium	onion finely chopped
1/4 cup	pine nuts
1 large	tomato finely diced
2 cups	tomato sauce

Sauté eggplants in olive oil for approximately 10 minutes. Remove with a slotted strainer. Let cool. Make a 2-inch slit in the middle of each eggplant. Add allspice, cinnamon and salt to ground beef and sauté in 2 tablespoon butter for 8 minutes. Add onion and sauté´ further for 5 minutes or until onion is limp. Separately, sauté pine nuts in 1 tablespoon butter. Eggplant filling is made by mixing meat/onion mixture, pine nuts and tomato well. Stuff eggplant with filling. Place in a pan and pour tomato sauce on top. Bake in preheated oven to 350°F for approximately 30-45 minutes or until eggplants are tender.

Estimated time of preparation: 15 minutes
Estimated time of cooking: 60 minutes

Baked Eggplant & Zucchini
(masbeHt al darweesh)

SERVES 6 | 278 calories per serving

1 pound	chuck beef, cubed
2 tablespoons	butter
1 large	onion, chopped
1 teaspoon	salt (optional)
1/2 teaspoon	ground allspice
1/4 teaspoon	cinnamon
4 large	tomatoes, peeled and diced
2 medium	potatoes, chopped
1 large	eggplant chopped
1 large	zucchini, chopped

In a pan sauté meat in butter until brown (approximately 8 minutes). Add onions, salt, allspice and cinnamon. Sauté until onions limp. Cover meat with water and simmer for 30 minutes until meat is tender. Remove meat and onions from pan with a slotted strainer and place on a baking pan. Add tomatoes, potatoes, eggplants and zucchini and 1/2 cup water. Bake in a preheated oven at 350°F until vegetables and meat are tender (30 minutes).

Estimated time of preparation: 20 minutes
Estimated time of cooking: 75 minutes

Poultry Dishes

Baked Chicken & Vegetable
(djaj mHammar ma' khudra)

SERVES 6 | 412 calories per serving

4-5 pounds	fryer chicken pieces, cut up
4 medium	potatoes, peeled and quartered
2 medium	onions, sliced
5 large	carrots, peeled and cut in 2-inch pieces
1 medium	zucchini, sliced
1/4 cup	olive oil
1 teaspoon	basil
1/2 teaspoon	salt (optional)
1/2 teaspoon	ground allspice

*Note: The chicken is either dipped, if desired, in garlic sauce
(toum bil zayt) served separately on the side, or basted with garlic
sauce while baking it.*

Preheat oven to 400°F. Place chicken that has been coated
with 1/2 of spice mixture on bottom of baking dish and add
vegetables that have been coated in olive oil and the other
half of spices on top. Bake for 1 hour or until chicken
is baked through.

Estimated time of preparation: 20 minutes
Estimated time of cooking: 60 minutes

Chicken & Rice
(riz ma' djaj)

SERVES 6
610 calories per serving

4-5 pounds	fryer chicken pieces, cut up
1 teaspoon	salt (optional)
2	onions
1/2 teaspoon	ground allspice
1/2 teaspoon	cinnamon
3/4 pound	ground beef
2 tablespoons	butter, divided
2 cups	rice, washed and drained (basmati works nicely)
1/2 cup	pine nuts and slivered almonds
4 cups	chicken broth, store bought or from cooking of chicken above

Place chicken, salt, onions, allspice, and cinnamon in a pan. Add water to just cover chicken. Bring to a boil, and then reduce to low   until cooked through (approximately 45 minutes). Set aside 4 cups chicken broth if not using store bought. In a separate sauce pan, sauté ground meat with one tablespoon of butter until brown. Add to it rice and chicken broth and heat to boil, then simmer under low heat until rice is tender (approximately 20-24 minutes). While rice is cooking, sauté pine nuts and almonds with 1 tablespoon of butter until golden. Place rice and ground beef mixture on a serving platter. Once boiled chicken is cool enough to handle, tear meat into bite size pieces. Add chicken on top of rice and then add nuts and almonds on top of chicken.

Estimated time of preparation: 20 minutes
Estimated time of cooking: 60 minutes

Pasta & Chicken with White Sauce
(macaroni ma' djaj)

SERVES 10 | 510 calories per serving

3 pounds	boneless chicken meat (5 pounds with bones)
1 teaspoon	salt (optional)
1/2 teaspoon	ground allspice
1/4 teaspoon	cinnamon
16 ounces	extra wide egg noodles
4 cups	store bought chicken broth or from boiled chicken above
2 cups	skim milk
3/4 cup	white flour
2 teaspoons	nutmeg powder
16 ounces	shredded gruyere or mozzarella cheese

Preheat oven to 350°F. Place chicken in a pan and add water to just cover chicken. Heat to boil. Add salt, allspice and cinnamon. Simmer chicken under medium heat for approximately 30 minutes until tender. Set aside 4 cups of chicken broth if not using store bought. Once chicken is cool enough to handle, shred chicken meat into bite size pieces. Prepare pasta in boiling water, according to package directions. Place pasta in a strainer and wash it with running cold water. To prepare the white sauce, mix 1 cup chicken broth, and flour in a plastic container with lid. Shake until mixed well. Add this to a separate sauce pan along with the milk, remaining 3 cups of chicken broth, and nutmeg. Whisk until sauce comes to a boil and thickens. Continue to boil 1 minute longer. Remove from heat. Spray bottom of 9" x 13" baking pan with cooking spray and place evenly 1/3 of the cooked pasta. Spread chicken on top of pasta and then pour 2 cups of sauce on top of chicken. Spread remaining pasta on chicken and pour remaining sauce on top. Place cheese evenly on top of pasta. You may add a couple of pinches of nutmeg to your taste evenly over the top of the dish. Bake for approximately 30 minutes or until bubbly. Broil 1-2 minutes until noodles and cheese become light brown.

Estimated time of preparation: 25 minutes
Estimated time of cooking: 70 minutes

Burghul with Chicken
(burghul ma' djaj)

SERVES 6 | 462 calories per serving

4-5 pounds	cubed chicken meat
1/4 cup	vegetable oil
1 medium	onion coarsely chopped
3 large	red tomatoes, skin peeled and coarsely chopped
1/2 teaspoon	salt (optional)
1/2 teaspoon	ground allspice
1/2 teaspoon	cinnamon
6 cups	water or chicken broth
2 cups	burghul
2 tablespoons	butter

Sauté chicken in oil under low heat until light brown
(approximately 20 minutes). Add onions and sauté for 6 more
minutes until onions are limp. Place chicken and onions in
a pan and add tomatoes, salt, allspice, cinnamon and 2 cups
of water or broth. Heat to boil then simmer under medium
heat for 10 minutes, or until water has evaporated. Drain
water. Add burghul, butter and 4 cups of water. Mix all
ingredients together. Heat to boil then simmer under medium
heat or until water evaporates (approximately 15 minutes).
Burghul is served on a platter with pickles and salads.

Estimated time of preparation: 10 minutes
Estimated time of cooking: 55 minutes

Moghrabieh* with Chicken
(moghrabieh ma' djaj)

SERVES 8 | 661 calories per serving

1 cup	dried garbanzo beans or 15 ounce can rinsed and drained
1 teaspoon	baking soda (omit if using canned beans)
4-5 pounds	skinless chicken breasts and thighs
2 teaspoons	ground allspice, divided
1 teaspoon	cinnamon, divided
1 teaspoon	salt (optional)
4-5 cups	chicken broth from cooked chicken above
1 pound	pearl or boiler onions, boiled in water for 3 min., removed, rinsed in cold water, ends cut off and skins removed
2 cups	dried moghrabieh product or couscous can be substituted
4 tablespoons	butter
1/2 teaspoon	caraway, divided

Moghrabieh is a semolina based product found in ethnic stores, and is known as large couscous.

Place garbanzo beans in a pan with 1 tsp. of baking soda. Cover with water and soak for 1 hour. Rinse garbanzo beans and drain.

Start here if using canned beans
Place chicken in a pan and water to just cover chicken. Add 1 tsp. allspice, 1/2 tsp. cinnamon, 1/4 tsp. caraway, and salt. Heat to boil and simmer under medium heat until chicken is tender (approximately 1 hour). Add beans and onions while cooking and remove only onions with a slotted spoon after 10 minutes or when tender. Set aside. Meanwhile soak moghrabieh in hot water for 30 minutes. Drain. In a deep pan, sauté moghrabieh with butter under low heat for 10 minutes

or until golden brown. While sautéing add remaining allspice, cinnamon, and caraway. After sautéing begin to add chicken broth (which was made when boiling chicken) to moghrabieh about 1/2 cup at a time and stir often. Test moghrabieh after broth has been added. When it is al Dante it is ready. Remove chicken and beans with a slotted spoon. Shred chicken into bite size pieces once it is cool enough to handle. On a serving platter place moghrabieh followed by chicken and garbanzo beans for the next layer. Finally, garnish with onions. You may add additional cinnamon, allspice, and caraway on top if you wish. Serve warm.

Estimated time of preparation: 20 minutes
Estimated time of cooking: 50 minutes

Barbecued Chicken
(shish tawook)

SERVES 6 | 403 calories per serving

1/2 cup	vinegar
1/2 cup	olive oil
1 tablespoon	tomato paste
1/4 teaspoon	ground allspice
1/4 teaspoon	black pepper
1 teaspoon	salt (optional)
2 pounds	boneless chicken breast, cubed

In a bowl mix vinegar, oil, tomato paste, allspice and salt. Soak chicken in the refrigerated mixture for 1/2 hour. Put the meat on a skewer and barbecue on grill. Serve with Arabic bread, pickles and salads.

Estimated time of preparation: 35 minutes
Estimated time of cooking: 25 minutes

Flavors of Lebanon |

Chicken & Bread Crumbs
(djaj ma' ka'k)

SERVES 6 | 506 calories per serving

2 pounds	boneless chicken breast (6-7 pieces)
1/4 cup	white flour
4 large	beaten eggs or equivalent egg beaters
1 teaspoon	salt (optional)
1/2 teaspoon	ground allspice
1/2 teaspoon	cinnamon
1 1/2 cups	bread crumbs
1 cup	vegetable oil
	(approximately 1/4 cup will be consumed)
1	lemon sliced into wedges

Wrap pieces of chicken with wax paper. Flatten with a mallet to 1/4 inch thickness. Combine beaten eggs, salt, allspice and cinnamon. Dip pieces into flour, then egg mixture, and then bread crumbs. Refrigerate for 30 minutes. In a saucepan, sauté chicken in oil under low to medium heat until chicken is tender and golden. Serve with lemon wedges.

Estimated time of preparation: 30 minutes
Estimated time of cooking: 20 minutes

Stuffed Chicken
(djaj meHshi)

SERVES 7 | 891 calories per serving

1/2 cup	regular white rice
1 cup	water
1 pound	ground lean beef meat
1/4 cup	butter, divided
1 teaspoon	salt (optional)
1 teaspoon	ground allspice
1/4 cup	pine nuts
1 whole	chicken (4 pounds)
1/2 cup	plain yogurt

Place rice in a pan and cover with 1 cup water.
Heat to boil then simmer under medium heat for
approximately 15 minutes. In a saucepan, sauté beef meat
with 2 tablespoons of butter until brown (approximately
10 minutes). Add salt, allspice and rice to meat and stir well
under medium heat. In a separate pan, sauté pine nuts with
2 tablespoon butter until golden. Add pine nuts to meat and
rice and mix well. Stuff inside chicken cavity with above
filling. Skew cavity openings. Place chicken in a pan and
cover with water. Heat to boil. Skim foam from surface of
liquid. Simmer under medium heat for approximately
15 minutes. Remove chicken from water. Brush with plain
yogurt. Cover with aluminum foil and bake in a preheated
oven to 350°F until chicken is brown (approximately
40 minutes).

Estimated time of preparation: 15 minutes
Estimated time of cooking: 90 minutes

Flavors of Lebanon

Mlukhiyyi with Chicken
(mlukhiyyi bil djaj)

SERVES 8 | 540 calories per serving

4-5 pounds	cut up fryer chicken
8 cups	chicken broth from boiling chicken above
2 teaspoons	salt (optional), divided
1/2 teaspoon	cinnamon
1 teaspoon	ground allspice, divided
2 medium	onions finely chopped, divided
10 cloves	garlic
1 bunch	fresh cilantro leaves or 2 Tbsp. dried coriander
1/4 cup	butter
1/4 cup	fresh squeezed lemon juice
4 medium	onions, baked in oven at 350°F until limp and then finely chopped
2 pounds	fresh* mlukhiyyi leaves coarsely chopped
1/2 cup	vinegar
4 large	Arabic pita breads baked in oven until light brown and broken into 1 inch pieces
1 recipe	rice pilaf (page 107)

Canned or frozen mlukhiyyi may also be used.

Place chicken in a pan and add water to just cover chicken.
Add 1 teaspoon salt. Heat to boil. Simmer under medium
heat until tender (approximately 50 minutes). Skim foam
from surface of liquid as it accumulates. Add cinnamon,

allspice and 1 medium onion to chicken while cooking. Chicken is then removed and shredded into bite size pieces once it is cool enough to handle. Save chicken broth in a pan for later use. Mix in food processor garlic, cilantro, baked onions, 1 teaspoon salt. Move the garlic/cilantro/onion mixture to a deep pan. Sauté in butter under medium heat for approximately 5 minutes. Add lemon juice and mlukhiyyi to this mixute and continue to sauté for 5 minutes. Add remaining chicken broth a few cups at a time until you reach the consistency and taste you desire. It will be the consistency of a soup. Cover pan and simmer for 5 minutes. Mlukhiyyi is then placed in a large serving bowl. Chicken is placed on a platter. Baked Arabic bread is placed in a serving bowl, as well as the rice pilaf. In 2 smaller separate bowls, mix chopped fresh onions and vinegar, and chopped fresh onions and lemon juice. When serving, place baked bread pieces first, followed by rice pilaf then mlukhiyyi and then chicken. On top, pour vinegar/onion mixture or lemon/onion mixture to taste.

Estimated time of preparation: 15 minutes
Estimated time of cooking: 40 minutes

Chicken with Curry
(djaj ma' curry)

SERVES 6 | 666 calories per serving

2 pounds	boneless chicken breasts
1 teaspoon	salt (optional)
2 medium	onions, skin peeled and coarsely chopped
1/2 teaspoon	ground allspice
12 ounces	spaghetti
8 ounces	grated gruyere cheese
2 teaspoons	curry
2 tablespoons	white flour
2 tablespoons	butter

Place chicken and salt in a pan. Add enough water to just cover the chicken. Heat to boil. Add onions and allspice. Cover and simmer under medium heat until chicken is tender (approximately 30-40 minutes). Skim foam from surface of liquid as it accumulates. Chicken is then removed. Chicken broth is filtered in a strainer and placed in a separate pan. Add pasta to broth. Simmer under medium heat until pasta is tender (approximately 10-15 minutes). Remove pasta a place it on a serving plate. Sprinkle cheese on top. Add curry, flour, and butter to remaining chicken broth and mix well with a whisk. Simmer under low heat while stirring until sauce is thick. Place chicken on top of pasta and pour sauce on top.

Estimated time of preparation: 15 minutes
Estimated time of cooking: 60 minutes

Stuffed Turkey
(Habash meHshi)

SERVES 12 | 845 calories per serving

2 pounds	ground lean beef meat
4 tablespoons	butter, divided
1 1/2 teaspoons	ground allspice
1 teaspoon	salt (optional)
1 cup	regular white rice
1/4 cup	pine nuts
1/2 cup	slivered almonds
9 pound	whole turkey

Sauté meat with 3 tablespoon butter until brown (approximately 10 minutes). Add allspice and salt to meat while sautéing. Add rice to meat and sauté for 5 more minutes. In a separate pan sauté pine nuts and almonds with 1 tablespoon butter until golden. Place meat/rice mixture, almonds and nuts in pan. Add 2 cups water. Heat to boil. Simmer under medium heat until rice is cooked and water evaporates (approximately 15 minutes). Fill inside turkey cavity with stuffing. Skew cavity openings. Place turkey in a pan and cover with aluminum foil. Bake at 350°F for approximately 3 and 1/2 hours. Remove foil and cook further until meat is cooked thoroughly to 180 degrees fahrenheit.

Estimated time of preparation: 20 minutes
Estimated time of cooking: 4 and 1/2 hours

Chicken with White Sauce
(djaj ma' salsa bayda)

SERVES 6 | 647 calories per serving

1 1/2 pounds	boneless chicken meat
1 cup	vegetable oil (only 1/4 cup consumed)
3 large	carrots, skin peeled, julienne into 2 inch long pieces
1 small	onion coarsely chopped
2 medium	potatoes, skin peeled and sliced into 1/4 inch thick pieces
8 ounces	fresh mushrooms
1/2 teaspoon	salt (optional)
1/2 teaspoon	ground allspice
3 cups	water
1 cup	chicken broth saved from cooking above
4 tablespoons	butter
4 tablespoons	all purpose white flour
1 cup	skim milk
1/4 cup	finely chopped parsley leaves or 1 tablespoon dried and minced parsley

In a saucepan, fry chicken in oil under low heat until light brown (approximately 20 minutes). Remove chicken and place in a pan. In the remaining oil, sauté carrots, onions, potatoes, and mushrooms (approximately 7 minutes). Add these vegetables, salt and allspice to chicken. Add 3 cups water. Heat to boil. Simmer under medium heat until vegetables are tender (approximately 20 minutes). Save chicken broth. In a separate sauce pan mix butter and flour to form roux. Stir for a few minutes. Add milk and chicken broth. Mix well with a whisk. Simmer under medium heat while continuously stirring until a thick sauce is formed. Place chicken and vegetables on a serving plate and pour white sauce over it. Sprinkle parsley on top.

Estimated time of preparation: 15 minutes
Estimated time of cooking: 70 minutes

Chicken & Wheat Kernels
(hresat al djaj)

SERVES 6 | 476 calories per serving

3 pounds	cubed boneless chicken breast
7 cups	water
2 teaspoons	salt (optional)
1/2 teaspoon	ground allspice
1/2 teaspoon	cinnamon
1/2 cup	wheat berries
1/4 cup	melted butter

Place chicken in pan and cover with water or broth. Heat to boil. Remove foam from surface of liquid. Add salt, allspice, cinnamon and wheat berries to chicken. Simmer under low heat stirring frequently until a thick sauce is formed. Add butter on top and mix well. Remove from heat. Serve warm.

Estimated time of preparation: 15 minutes
Estimated time of cooking: 65 minutes

Fish Dishes

Fish & Rice
(sayadeyeh)

SERVES 9
824 calories per serving

3 pounds	halibut filets*
1 1/2 cups	vegetable oil
10 1/2 cups	water, divided
5 large	onions, thinly sliced
3 1/2 cups	instant white rice
1/2 cup	pine nuts
1 tablespoon	butter
1 1/2 teaspoons	salt (optional)
1/4 teaspoon	cumin
3 sticks	cinnamon

white or sword fish may be substituted

Salt fish. Fry in vegetable oil until golden. Remove with
a slotted spoon and place in a bowl. Let cool then tear into
small pieces. Remove oil from heat. In a pan, place 1/2 cup
of used oil and add to it 1/2 cup water. Sauté onions in
water/oil mixture until light brown. Remove onions with
a slotted spoon. Place in a food processor and coarsely
process. Strain all remaining oil and place in a pan. Add
10 cups of water along with onions and cinnamon sticks to
strained oil. Heat to boil. Add torn fish and simmer for 15
minutes. Remove fish and onions and place in a bowl. Add
rice to remaining water/oil mixture and cook for 10 minutes.
Rice is then removed, strained and placed on a serving plate.
Fish and onions are placed on top of rice. Sauté pine nuts
with 1 tablespoon butter until golden and sprinkle on top of
fish. Also Sprinkle cumin on top.

Estimated time of preparation: 30 minutes
Estimated time of cooking: 80 minutes

Fish & Onion
(tajin)

SERVES 6 | 642 calories per serving

2 pounds	halibut filets*
1 cup	vegetable oil
4 large	onions sliced
1 recipe	tahini with lemon (page 152)
1/2 teaspoon	hot white pepper (optional)

white or sword fish may be substituted

Fry fish in oil until golden. Remove fish with a strainer and place in a baking pan. Sauté onion in remaining oil until limp. Remove onion with a slotted spoon and place evenly over fish. Pour taratour over onions. Sprinkle pepper on top. Bake in oven for 10 to 15 minutes.

Estimated time of preparation: 10 minutes
Estimated time of cooking: 40 minutes

Baked Fish in Hot Sauce
(samak meshwee Har)

SERVES 10 | 684 calories per serving

6 pounds	halibut filets*
1 teaspoon	salt (optional)
10 cloves	garlic
1 stalk	green coriander
1/2 cup	vegetable oil
3/4 pound	walnuts, processed finely in a
1 recipe	tahini with lemon (page 152)
1/4 teaspoon	dried and ground jalapeno pepper
	food processor
lemon	garnish

white or sword fish may be substituted

Fish is salted and wrapped in aluminum foil and baked in
preheated oven to 350°F for 1/2 hour. Fish is then deboned,
torn into pieces and placed on a serving plate. Garlic and
coriander are mashed and sautéed for 3 minutes in oil.
Walnuts are then added to garlic and coriander and sautéed
for 3 more minutes. Taratour and jalapeno pepper are then
added to walnuts/garlic mixture while continuously stirring
under low heat until oil and taratour are mixed well. Pour
taratour/walnut mixture on baked fish. Decorate with 1/2
slices of lemon.

Estimated time of preparation: 20 minutes
Estimated time of cooking: 55 minutes

Flavors of Lebanon

Fried Fish
(samak meqlee)

SERVES 5 | 762 calories per serving

2 pounds	halibut filets
1 teaspoon	salt (optional)
1 cup	vegetable oil
1 pound	Arabic bread
1 recipe	tahini with lemon (page 152)

Salt fish then fry in oil. Remove with slotted spoon and place on a serving plate. Fry bread in same oil until brown. Remove with slotted spoon. Fish is served with fried bread and taratour as sauce.

Estimated time of preparation: 5 minutes
Estimated time of cooking: 30 minutes

Fish in Kibbi
(kibbet al samak)

SERVES 8 | 489 calories per serving

2 cups	burghul
2 pounds	halibut filets
1 stalk	green coriander, chopped
	or 1 tablespoon dried coriander
1 large	onion finely chopped and
2 large	onions coarsely chopped, divided
1 1/2 tablespoons	salt (optional)
1/2 teaspoon	ground allspice
1/4 teaspoon	cinnamon
3/4 cup	vegetable oil
1/4 cup	pine nuts

Soak burghul in cold water for 1/2 hour. Meanwhile, in a food processor process fish, coriander, 1 onion, salt, allspice and cinnamon. Knead burghul and fish together to form a firm dough. Add water as necessary. Coarsely chop the 2 remaining onions. Sauté onions in vegetable oil for 4 minutes. Add pine nuts to onions and sauté further until nuts are golden and onions are light brown. Spread onions/nuts mixture evenly on a 9x12" pan. Place dough on wax paper and roll it with a rolling pin. Make dough approximately 9x12" and place it over the onion/nut mixture. The wax paper is used to facilitate placement of dough over mixture. Dough is then spread evenly with fingers. Cut dough into squares. Pour remaining oil over top of dough and bake in preheated oven at 400°F for 40 minutes or until golden brown.

Estimated time of preparation: 30 minutes
Estimated time of cooking: 50 minutes

Shrimp in Avocado
(araydis ma' avocado)

SERVES 5 | 771 calories per serving

1 pound	small shrimps, shell-removed
2 cups	water
1 whole	small onion
2 sticks	cinnamon
2 tablespoons	fresh lemon juice
5 large	avocado
1/2 cup	shrimp sauce
1/2 cup	mayonnaise

Place shrimps in 2 cups water. Heat to boil. Add onion, cinnamon and lemon juice. Simmer for 8 minutes. Remove shrimps with a slotted spoon. Peel avocado skin. Slice in 1/2 and remove seed from inside. Inside each half place shrimp sauce/mayonnaise mixture and 4-5 small shrimps.
Serve as an appetizer.

Estimated time of preparation: 10 minutes
Estimated time of cooking: 12 minutes

Fish Dishes

Vegetarian Dishes

Lebanese Omelet
(ijji)

SERVES 7 | 305 calories per serving

8 medium	eggs or equivalent egg substitute
1/4 teaspoon	cinnamon
1/2 teaspoon	salt (optional)
1/4 teaspoon	ground allspice
1 medium	onion diced
1/2 cup	chopped parsley leaves
3/4 cup	all-purpose flour
1/4 cup	skim milk
1/2 cup	olive oil

Mix eggs, cinnamon, salt, allspice, milk, onions, parsley and flour well in a food processor. Place a thin layer of olive oil in a pan and heat at medium heat. Slowly, pour omelet mixture (approximately 1/4 cup each) over the heated pan and cook until light brown (approximately 5-7 minutes). Turn ijji over to cook the other side.

Estimated time of preparation: 10 minutes
Estimated time of cooking: 35 minutes

Rice Pilaf
(riz mfalfal)

SERVES 6
198 calories per serving

1/2 cup	vermicelli
1 tablespoon	butter
2 cups	water
1 cup	regular white rice
1 teaspoon	salt (optional)

Sauté vermicelli with butter under low heat, stirring
continuously until golden brown. Add water to vermicelli.
Heat water to boil. Add rice, salt and stir. Lower heat to
simmer. Cover pan and cook rice and vermicelli for
15-20 minutes. Do not stir rice or take of lid while cooking.

Estimated time of preparation: 5 minutes
Estimated time of cooking: 25 minutes

Chickpeas Dip
(Hommus bil tahini)

SERVES 10
224 calories per serving

2 cups	dried garbanzo beans or two 15 ounce cans
1/2 teaspoon	baking soda (omit if using canned beans)
2 teaspoons	salt (optional), divided
1/2 cup	tahini
1/2 cup	lemon juice
1 clove	garlic

Cover garbanzo beans with boiling water and add baking soda. Let soak for 2 hours, then wash chick peas under cold running water. Place soaked peas in a pan and cover with water. Add 1 teaspoon salt and boil for approximately 90 minutes (or until peas are cooked). Omit the above steps if using canned beans. Drain garbanzo beans and place in a food processor. Add tahini, lemon juice, garlic and 1 teaspoon salt. Process for 3-5 minutes until a smooth paste is obtained. Add water as needed during processing to achieve desired paste consistency (approximately 1 and 1/2 cups). Hommus is spread on a platter and a sprinkle of olive oil is usually added to it.

Estimated time of preparation: 10 minutes
Estimated time of cooking: 100 minutes

Rice & Curry
(riz bil curry)

SERVES 4 | 235 calories per serving

2 medium	onions chopped
1 large	green pepper chopped
1 tablespoon	butter
1 medium	tomato chopped
1/2 teaspoon	salt (optional)
3/4 tablespoon	curry
2 cups	water
1 cup	regular white rice
1 cup	green peas

Sauté onions and green pepper in butter under medium heat for approximately 8 minutes or until onions are limp. Add tomato, salt, curry. Sauté for 5 more minutes. Meanwhile, in a heavy pan, heat water to boil then add rice and green peas to boiling water. Lower heat to simmer. Cover pan and let rice and peas cook for approximately 14-20 minutes. Do not stir while rice and peas are cooking. Add onions, green pepper and tomato on top of cooked rice and peas. Serve warm.

Estimated time of preparation: 10 minutes
Estimated time of cooking: 30 minutes

Green Bean Stew
(lubieh bil zayt)

SERVES 6
225 calories per serving

1 large	onion, diced
4 cloves	garlic, crushed
1/2 cup	olive oil
2 1/2 pounds	green beans, washed, drained, ends snipped and cut into 2 inch long pieces
1 teaspoon	salt (optional)
1/2 teaspoon	ground allspice
3/4 teaspoon	cinnamon
4 cups	water
2 large	tomatoes diced or 15 ounce can chopped tomatoes

In a saucepan, sauté onions and garlic in oil for approximately 6 minutes under medium heat or until onions limp. Add beans, salt, allspice and cinnamon and sauté for 5 more minutes. Add water. Cover pan and simmer under medium heat for 40 minutes. Add tomatoes, stir and cook for 10 more minutes or until beans are tender. Serve with rice pilaf.

Estimated time of preparation: 15 minutes
Estimated time of cooking: 65 minutes

Lentils with Rice
(mjadra bil riz)

SERVES 6
453 calories per serving

1 1/2 cups	dried lentils, washed and drained
5 cups	water
1 teaspoon	salt (optional)
1 cup	regular white rice
2 large	onions, chopped
1/2 cup	vegetable oil

Place lentils in a pan. Add water and salt. Heat to boil.
Cover and simmer under medium heat until lentils are tender
(approximately 20 minutes). Add rice to lentils, bring to a boil
and simmer for 24 minutes or until rice and lentils are tender
and water is absorbed. Meanwhile, sauté onion with oil until
light brown. Pour onions and oil over cooked lentils and rice
and mix well. Served with Arabic bread, plain yogurt, green
onions or garden variety salad.

Estimated time of preparation: 10 minutes
Estimated time of cooking: 65 minutes

Vegetarian Dishes

Fava Beans with Lemon Juice
(foul madamas)

SERVES 4 | 305 calories per serving

1 cup	dried fava beans
3 cloves	garlic
1 teaspoon	salt (optional)
1/4 cup	freshly squeezed lemon juice
1/2 teaspoon	ground allspice
1/4 cup	olive oil
1/2 cup	finely chopped parsley leaves for garnish

Soak fava beans overnight. Wash and drain. Place in a pan and cover with water. Heat to boil. Cover and simmer beans under medium heat for approximately 70 minutes or until beans are tender. Meanwhile, mash garlic with salt. Add to garlic lemon juice, allspice, and oil. Drain fava beans from water. In a bowl, mix garlic mixture and fava beans. Sprinkle parsley on top. Serve while warm with Arabic bread and green onion.

Estimated time of preparation: 10 minutes
Estimated time of cooking: 70 minutes

Roasted Cauliflower
(arnabeet meshwee)

SERVES 3 | 240 calories per serving

> 1 large   cauliflower (approximately 2 pounds)
> 1/4 cup   vegetable oil
> 1/2 teaspoon   salt (optional)

Cut cauliflower into 1 and 1/2 inch pieces. Wash and drain.
Place cauliflower in a pan and cover with water. Heat to boil.
Parboil under low heat for approximately 5 minutes. Drain
water. Salt cauliflower and place in a baking pan. Brush top
with oil. Preheat oven to 400°F. Bake for approximately 20
minutes or until light brown. Serve with Arabic bread and
taratour sauce.

Estimated time of preparation: 10 minutes
Estimated time of cooking: 30 minutes

Kibbet Raheb
(kibbet raheb)

SERVES 8 | 557 calories per serving

1 1/2 cups	burghul
1 cup	white flour
1 1/2 cups	parsley leaves finely chopped
1 1/2 cups	green mint leaves finely chopped or
	1 1/2 tablespoon dried mint leaves
3/4 tablespoon	ground allspice
1 large	onion finely chopped
1 1/2 cups	lentils
8 cups	water
6 cloves	garlic
1 teaspoon	salt (optional)
1 cup	olive oil
3 tablespoons	sumac (optional)

Soak burghul for 10 minutes in water. Drain water and add flour, parsley, 1 cup of fresh mint, allspice and onions. Water is added as necessary until a firm dough is formed. Make dough into 1/2 inch spheres using palms of both hands. Place spheres on a tray. Meanwhile place lentils in a pan and cover with 8 cups of water. Heat to boil. Parboil under medium fire (approximately 20 minutes). Mash garlic with salt. Add garlic, 1/2 cup of fresh mint, olive oil, sumac and spheres to lentils and simmer until both lentils and spheres are cooked (approximately 30 minutes). Serve hot or cold.

Estimated time of preparation: 40 minutes
Estimated time of cooking: 60 minutes

Flavors of Lebanon |

Baked Eggplant with Tahini
(baba ghanouj)

SERVES 7 | 186 calories per serving

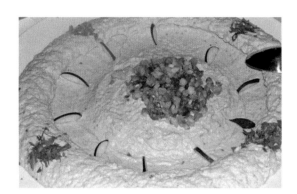

2 large	eggplants (2 pounds)
4 cloves	garlic
1/2 teaspoon	salt (optional)
1/2 cup	lemon juice
1/2 cup	tahini
2 tablespoons	olive oil
1/4 cup	chopped parsley leaves

Barbecue eggplants then peel off skin while warm under running cold water. Cut eggplant in half along its length and remove seeds. Mash garlic and salt. In a food processor place eggplant, garlic, lemon juice and tahini. Process for 1 to 2 minutes. Spread eggplant mix on a large serving plate and sprinkle oil on top. Garnish with parsley. Serve with pickles and Arabic bread.

Estimated time of preparation: 10 minutes
Estimated time of cooking: 25 minutes

Baked Eggplant
(batinjan meshwee)

SERVES 6 | 82 calories per serving

2 large	eggplants (2 pounds)
3 cloves	garlic
1/2 teaspoon	salt (optional)
2 tablespoons	olive oil
1/4 cup	chopped parsley leaves

Barbecue eggplants and peel off skin while warm under running cold water. Cut eggplant in half along its length and remove seeds. Cut eggplant into 1/2 inch pieces. Mash garlic and salt. Add garlic and oil to eggplant and mix well. Place on a plate and garnish with parsley.

Estimated time of preparation: 10 minutes
Estimated time of cooking: 25 minutes

Green Okra with Tomato
(bami bil banadoura)

SERVES 8 | 414 calories per serving

2 pounds	green okra* tops removed, washed and drained
1 cup	olive oil
2 large	onions thinly sliced
1 tablespoon	dried coriander
5 cloves	garlic, crushed
2 large	tomatoes, skin peeled and diced or two 15 ounce cans chopped tomatoes
1 teaspoon	salt (optional)
1/4 teaspoon	ground allspice
1/4 cup	fresh lemon juice
2 cups	water

if dried okra is used, 4 ounces is needed. Place dried okra in boiling water for 10 minutes. Remove into a strainer and let dry. Okra can now be used with above recipe. Frozen okra may also be used.

Sauté okra with oil until light brown (approximately 20 minutes). Remove from oil with a slotted spoon and place in a pan. Sauté onions with oil used for okra until limp. Add coriander and garlic to onions and sauté for 2 more minutes. Remove with a slotted spoon and add to okra. Add tomato, salt, pepper, lemon and water to okra. Mix and simmer under medium fire for approximately 40 minutes or until okra is tender.

Estimated time of preparation: 20 minutes
Estimated time of cooking: 70 minutes

Falafel
(falafel)

SERVES 10

414 calories per serving

1 cup	skinless dried broad beans
1/2 cup	dried chickpeas
3 cloves	garlic
1 medium	onion
1 teaspoon	dried coriander
1 teaspoon	salt (optional)
1 teaspoon	baking powder
1/2 teaspoon	ground allspice
1/4 teaspoon	ground cinnamon
1/4 teaspoon	ground cumin
2 tablespoons	all-purpose flour
3 cups	vegetable oil (only 1/4 cup will be consumed)

Soak beans and chickpeas for 24 hours. Drain water well and place in a food processor. Add garlic, onion, coriander, salt, baking powder, allspice, cinnamon and cumin and flour and process well. Place in a mixing bowl. Knead well. Allow falafel dough to rest for 1/2 hour. In a frying pan place oil and heat well. Make dough into 1 inch spheres and fry in oil until medium brown. Serve with Arabic bread, taratour, tomatoes, and pickles.

Estimated time of preparation: 80 minutes
Estimated time of cooking: 25 minutes

Lentils with Burghul
(mjadra bil burghul)

SERVES 6 | 446 calories per serving

1 1/2 cups	dried lentils, washed and drained
5 cups	water
1/2 teaspoon	salt (optional)
1 cup	medium burghul
2 large	onions coarsely chopped
1/2 cup	vegetable oil

Place lentils in a pan. Add water and salt. Heat to boil.
Cover and simmer under medium heat until lentils are tender
(approximately 30 minutes). Add burghul over lentils and
stir. Simmer for 20 minutes under low heat. Do not cover
while simmering. Meanwhile, sauté onions with oil until light
brown. Pour onions and oil over lentils and burghul and mix
well. Simmer until water evaporates. Served with pickles,
salads or green onions.

Estimated time of preparation: 5 minutes
Estimated time of cooking: 65 minutes

Vegetarian Dishes

Drained Lentils
(mjadra msefayeh)

SERVES 6 | 456 calories per serving

1/2 cup	rice
2 cups	lentils
7 cups	water
1 teaspoon	salt (optional)
2 small	onions finely chopped
1/2 cup	vegetable oil

Place rice in a pan and cover with water. Heat to boil.
Cover pan and simmer under medium heat while stirring
continuously until rice is tender (approximately 15 minutes).
Meanwhile, place lentils in a pan and cover with 5 cups of
water. Heat to boil. Cover pan and simmer lentils under
medium heat until lentils are tender and skin appears peeling
off (approximately 30 minutes). Drain. Process lentils
in food processor. Add drained rice and salt to lentils and
process further for few more minutes. Sauté onions in oil
until light brown. Add onions and oil to lentils and rice
and process for 2 more minutes. Served with salad and
Arabic bread.

Estimated time of preparation: 15 minutes
Estimated time of cooking: 30 minutes

Stuffed Cabbage Leaves
(meHshi selik)

SERVES 7 | 329 calories per serving

1 1/2 cups	white rice
1 1/2 pounds	cabbage* leaves, washed and spread over a dry towel with a sprinkle of salt on every leaf
3/4 cup	parsley leaves, snipped and finely chopped
2 teaspoons	dried mint
1 large	onion coarsely chopped
2 large	red tomatoes, skin peeled and chopped
1/2 cup	oil
1/4 cup	lemon juice
1/2 teaspoon	ground allspice
1 teaspoon	salt (optional)

Swiss Chard leaves can be substituted.

In a bowl mix rice, parsley, mint, onion, tomatoes, oil, lemon juice, and allspice. Place stuffing in the center of each cabbage leaf. Fold edges to the center and roll leaves firmly in a cylinder. In a pan place stuffed cabbage in alternating layers starting from the outer rim of the pan to its center. Place a glass plate on top of stuffed leaves to prevent them from unfolding during cooking. Add 3 cups of water and 1 teaspoon salt to pan. Heat to boil. Simmer under low heat for 15 minutes or until rice is cooked.

Estimated time of preparation: 60 minutes
Estimated time of cooking: 20 minutes

Cooked Red Beans
(fasoulia Hamra)

SERVES 6 | 403 calories per serving

2 cups	red dry beans, washed and drained
4 cups	water
1 large	onion coarsely chopped
1/2 cup	olive oil
5 cloves	garlic mashed with dash of salt
1 teaspoon	salt (optional)
1/2 teaspoon	ground allspice

Soak beans in water for 4 hours. Drain and place in a pan.
Cover with 4 cups of water. Heat to boil. Cover and simmer
under medium heat until tender (approximately 35 minutes).
Sauté onion in oil until limp (approximately 8 minutes).
Add onions/oil mixture, garlic, salt, and allspice to beans.
Simmer for 20 more minutes. Serve with Arabic bread and
green onions.

Estimated time of preparation: 5 minutes
Estimated time of cooking: 70 minutes

Stuffed Grape Leaves
(meHshi waraq einab syami)

SERVES 8 | 306 calories per serving

100	green grape leaves
1 large	onion finely diced
1/2 teaspoon	ground allspice
1 large	tomato diced
1 tablespoon	dry mint
1 bunch	fresh parsley, finely chopped
2 cups	regular rice
2 teaspoons	salt (optional)
1/2 cup	vegetable oil
1/4 cup	freshly squeezed lemon juice
4 cups	lemon juice for cooking

Soak grape leaves in hot water for 10 minutes. Drain and let cool. Meanwhile mix onion, allspice, tomatoes, mint, parsley, oil, lemon juice and rice. In the bottom 1/3 of each grape leaf place 1 teaspoon of filling. Fold edges of leaves toward the center and firmly roll leaves upward into cylinders. Place cylinders in alternating layers starting from outer edge of a saucepan to its center. Sprinkle in salt. Place a glass plate on top of stuffed grape leaves to keep them from unfolding during cooking. Add water to just cover the leaves. Heat to boil then cover pan and simmer under low heat for 1-3 hours until tender. Toward the end of the cooking time add lemon juice 1/2 cup at time until desired taste is achieved.

Estimated time of preparation: 75 minutes
Estimated time of cooking: 50 minutes

Spaghetti in White Sauce
(macaroni bil Halib)

SERVES 10 | 382 calories per serving

1 teaspoon	oil
1 teaspoon	salt (optional)
1 pound	spaghetti
12 ounces	gruyere cheese, finely grated or mozzarella
2 recipes	white sauce (page)
1/2 teaspoon	nutmeg
1/2 cup	bread crumbs

Heat water in a pan. Add salt and oil to boiling water then spaghetti. Simmer under medium heat for 15 minutes. Stir occasionally while spaghetti is cooking . Remove from heat, place in a strainer and cool under running cold water. Once cooled, place evenly in a 9x12 inch pan. Sprinkle gruyere cheese on top then pour white sauce with nutmeg added evenly on top of spaghetti. Sprinkle bread crumbs on top. Bake in preheated oven at 400°F until bread crumbs are golden (approximately 25 minutes).

Estimated time of preparation: 5 minutes
Estimated time of cooking: 50 minutes

Desserts & Beverages

Basic Syrup
(ater)

Makes 2 cups | 372 calories per cup

2 cups	sugar
1 cup	water
1 tablespoon	fresh lemon juice
1 tablespoon	orange blossom or rose water (optional)

Mix sugar and water. Heat to boil. Simmer under medium heat for approximately 10 minutes. While simmering add lemon juice. To test whether syrup is ready, place 1 teaspoon on a plate and let cool. Syrup drop will stick on finger. Rose water or orange blossom water is then added to basic syrup.

Time of preparation: 15 minutes

Ma'moul with Semolina
(ma'moul bil smeed)

SERVES 29 | 288 calories per serving
(2 pieces per serving)

2 teaspoons	active yeast
1 cup	warm milk
3/4 cup	sugar
7 cups	semolina
1 1/2 cups	melted unsalted butter
1/2 cup	rose water (optional)
1/2 cup	orange blossom water
1 tablespoon	maHlab
1/2 cup	powdered sugar

Dissolve yeast in milk. In a bowl mix and knead well sugar, semolina, butter, rose water, orange blossom water and maHlab. Let soft dough sit for 30 minutes. Separate dough into 1 and 1/2 inches spheres. Place sphere on a wooden mold (called aleb or tabi') and press gently. Tap wooden mold on a plastic bag to separate dough. Ma'moul pieces are placed on an ungreased pan. Allow 1 inch space between each piece. Preheat oven to 350°F and bake ma'moul for approximately 15 to 20 minutes until light golden in color. Remove from oven and sprinkle powdered sugar on every piece.

Time of preparation: 90 minutes
Time of cooking: 20 minutes

Ma'moul with Walnuts*
(ma'moul bil jawz)

SERVES 29 | 447 calories per serving
(2 pieces per serving)

1 recipe	Ma'moul with semolina (page 129)
16 ounces	walnuts finely chopped
3/4 cup	sugar
3 tablespoons	orange blossom water
1/4 cup	unsalted butter

**Dates can be substituted for walnuts. Dates filling is prepared as follows: 20 ounce mashed dates mixed well with 1/2 cup melted unsalted butter (Ma'moul bil tamr)

Mix walnut, sugar and orange blossom water well. Separate ma'moul with semolina dough into 1 and 1/2 inches spheres. Using forefinger create a hole in every sphere. Place one teaspoon of walnut filling into cavity made. Close dough carefully. Place sphere on a wooden mold (called aleb or tabi') and press gently. Tap wooden mold on a plastic bag to separate dough. Ma'moul pieces are placed on an ungreased pan. Allow 1 inch space between every piece. Preheat oven to 350°F and bake ma'moul for 20 minutes until light golden in color. Remove from oven and sprinkle powdered sugar on every piece.

Time of preparation: 2 and 1/2 hrs.
Time of cooking: 20 minutes

Awwaymat Sweet
(awwaymat)

SERVES 30 | 237 calories per serving

1 package	dry active yeast
1 teaspoon	sugar
2 cups	warm water, divided
3 cups	flour
5 cups	vegetable oil
2 recipes	basic syrup (page 128)

Dissolve yeast and sugar in 1/2 cup warm water. Let sit for 10 minutes. In a bowl place flour, 1 and 1/2 cups water and yeast and mix well. Allow soft dough to rise (2 to 3 hours). Drop several dough pieces, one teaspoon-size each, into a deep fat fryer with enough oil to cover dough entirely. Dough pieces are fried until golden brown. Remove with a slotted spoon and place immediately in basic syrup for few minutes.

Time of preparation: 90 minutes
Time of cooking: 60 minutes

Semolina Squares
(nammoura)

SERVES 15 | 255 calories per serving

1/2 cup	unsalted melted butter, divided
3 cups	semolina
1 1/2 cups	plain yogurt
1 1/2 teaspoons	baking powder
1/2 cup	sugar
1/4 cup	blanched almonds
1 1/4 cups	basic syrup (page 128)

Grease a 9x12 inch pan with 1 tablespoon butter. Mix
semolina, yogurt, remaining butter, baking powder and sugar
well. Spread dough evenly on pan. With a knife, cut dough
through half thickness into 2 inches squares. Place one
almond in center of each square and press it half way into
dough. Bake in preheated oven at 350°F for approximately
25 minutes. Remove from oven and cut squares through full
dough thickness. Bake for 10 more minutes or until dough
is golden brown. Broil for approximately 1 minute. Remove
from oven and immediately pour cold basic syrup on top. Let
cool at room temperature before serving.

Time of preparation: 10 minutes
Time of cooking: 55 minutes

Flavors of Lebanon

Baklava
(baklava)

SERVES 35 | 192 calories per serving (1 piece per serving)

12 ounces	fillo dough (1 package=16 ounces)
3 cups	finely chopped walnuts and pistachios
3/4 cup	sugar
1 1/4 cups	unsalted butter
1 recipe	basic syrup (page 128)

Defrost fillo dough overnight in the refrigerator or for 4 hours at room temperature. In a bowl mix walnuts, pistachios (finely chopped in food processor) and sugar. Half the sheets of fillo dough should be spread on the bottom of a 10x15 inch pan. Using a scissors cut the fillo dough to fit the 10x15 inch pan. Coat the bottom layer of the pan with melted butter. Each sheet should be brushed with melted butter before the other sheet is layered on top. Walnuts and pistachios are evenly spread over the first half of fillo dough sheets. The top half of fillo dough is then layered over nuts similarly to the bottom half with each layer brushed with melted butter. The top layer should be also brushed with butter. With a knife, cut fillo dough through full thickness into 2x2 inch squares. Preheat oven to 300°F. Bake for approximately 1 hour. Do not broil. Remove from oven and saturate baklava with 2 cups of cold basic syrup. Allow 2 hours to cool at room temperature before removing pieces from pan.

Time of preparation: 75 minutes

Time of baking: 1 hour

Ka'k
(ka'k)

SERVES 32 | 220 calories per serving
(2 pieces per serving)

1/2 teaspoon	active yeast
1/4 cup	water
1/2 teaspoon	sugar
9 cups	flour
1 1/2 cups	sugar
1 cup	warm milk
4 large	eggs
1/2 cup	unsalted melted butter
1/2 teaspoon	baking powder

Mix yeast, 1/4 cup water and 1/2 teaspoon sugar. Let sit for 5 minutes. In a food processor mix flour, sugar, milk, eggs, butter, yeast and baking powder until dough is formed. Knead dough for a few more minutes with hands. Allow dough to rise in a warm place for 30 minutes. Divide dough into 1 and 1/2 inches spheres. Roll spheres into 6 inch long cylinders. Shape cylinders in a ring. Press ends of each cylinder together. Place dough rings on a baking sheet sprayed with oil. Bake in preheated oven to 400°F until golden brown (15-20 minutes).

Time of preparation: 45 minutes
Time of cooking: 15 minutes

Butter Cookies
(ghraybi)

SERVES 24 | 150 calories per serving

1 cup	sugar
1 cup	unsalted soft butter
2 cups	flour
1/4 cup	blanched almonds

In a mixer mix well (for approximately 5 minutes) sugar and butter. Pour mixture on flour and knead with hands until a smooth dough is formed. Shape dough as desired (spheres or cylinders). A blanched almond can be placed in the middle of each cookie and slightly pressed into dough. Place on a baking sheet. Bake in a preheated oven to 300°F for approximately 12 minutes. Remove from oven. Allow to cool well before removing ghraybi from pan.

Time of preparation: 10 minutes
Time of cooking: 12 minutes

Caramel Cream
(creme caramel)

SERVES 10 | 192 calories per serving

1 cup	sugar
3 1/2 cups	2% milk
4 large	eggs
6 tablespoons	sugar
2 teaspoons	vanilla
1 lemon	peel grated

Place 1 cup sugar in a baking dish and heat over low fire until sugar melts and is light brown. Immediately, coat sides and bottom of baking dish with hot melted sugar using a spoon. Remove from heat. Mix well milk, eggs, sugar, vanilla and grated lemon peel using a mixer. Pour mix over coated baking dish. Bake in a preheated oven at 350°F for approximately 45 to 60 minutes until a toothpick into the dessert comes out clean. Cool at room temperature then refrigerate for 5 hours. Served cool with melted caramel as sauce.

Time of preparation: 10 minutes
Time of cooking: 60 minutes

Rice Pudding with Milk
(riz bil Halib)

SERVES 6 | 314 calories per serving

3/4 cup	regular white rice
3 cups	water
2 1/2 cups	2% milk, warm
1 cup	sugar
2 tablespoons	orange blossom water
1/2 cup	finely chopped pistachio

In a pan place rice and water. Heat to boil. Cover pan and simmer at low to medium heat for 15 minutes. Add warm milk and sugar to rice and simmer for approximately 25 minutes while stirring continuously with a whisk until a thick pudding is formed. Remove from heat. Add orange blossom water and mix well. Pour into cups and refrigerate. Pistachios are then sprinkled on top before serving.

Time of cooking: 60 minutes

Mhallabieh

(mhallabieh)

SERVES 6 | 326 calories per serving

3/4 cup	powdered rice
3 cups	water
3 cups	2% milk, warm
1/2 cup	sugar
2 tablespoons	orange blossom water
1 recipe	basic syrup* (page 128)

honey can be substituted

In a pan, place rice and water. Heat to boil. Lower heat to medium and simmer for 5 minutes while stirring constantly to prevent rice from sticking to bottom of pan. Add warm milk and simmer for 5 to 10 more minutes. Add sugar and orange blossom water and mix well for 1 or 2 minutes. Pour into cups and refrigerate. Basic syrup or honey is poured on top as desired prior to serving.

Time of cooking: 20 minutes

Ashtalieh
(ashtalieh)

SERVES 6 | 363 calories per serving

3/4 cup	corn starch
3 cups	water
3 cups	2% milk, warm
1 cup	sugar
1 tablespoon	orange blossom water
1 tablespoon	rose water
1 recipe	basic syrup (page 128)

In a pan place corn starch and water. Heat to boil. Lower heat to medium and simmer for 3-4 minutes while stirring constantly to prevent starch from sticking to bottom of pan. Add milk and sugar and simmer for approximately 10 minutes until thick pudding is formed. Add orange blossom and rose water and mix well. Pour into cups and refrigerate. Basic syrup is poured on top as desired prior to serving.

Time of cooking: 20 minutes

Baked Suzettes with Filling
(atayef)

SERVES 7 | 433 calories per serving

1/2 teaspoon	active yeast
1 1/2 cups	warm water, divided
2 cups	flour
1	egg
1/4 cup	sugar
1/2 teaspoon	salt
	cooking oil spray
2 recipes	basic syrup (page 128)
2 tablespoons	butter

Dissolve yeast in 1/2 cup warm water. In a separate bowl using a whisk mix flour, eggs, sugar, salt, yeast and 1 cup of warm water well (atayef mix). Let sit for 90 minutes. Spray frying pan with cooking oil spray. Place on medium heat. Pour 1/4 cup of atayef mix on the pan in a circular shape. Cook one side until light brown. Do not turn atayef pancakes over. Remove from pan. Place 1 teaspoon of filling (described below) in the center of the uncooked side of the pancake and fold in middle. Press edges together firmly. Place stuffed pancake on a greased pan with butter and bake in a preheated oven to 400°F for approximately 10 minutes. Pour 2 to 3 tablespoons of Basic syrup over each atayef pancake prior to serving. Atayef pancakes can also be fried in oil instead of baked in the oven.

Fillings:

1. Sweet cheese curds or Ricotta Cheese (1 pound) mixed with 1/2 cup sugar

2. 1/2 pound walnuts finely chopped mixed with 2 Tbsp. sugar

Time of preparation: 10 minutes
Time of cooking: 15 minutes

Spiced Rice Pudding
(mighli)

SERVES 8 | 345 calories per serving

1 teaspoon	anise seeds
8 1/2 cups	water, divided
1 cup	powdered white rice
2 cups	sugar
1 teaspoon	caraway
1 teaspoon	cinnamon
1/2 cup	dried grated coconut
1/2 cup	blanched almonds and pine nuts

Boil anise seeds in 1/2 cup water for 3 minutes. Drain water and save. Discard seeds. In a pan, mix well 8 cups water, powdered rice, sugar, anise water, caraway and cinnamon. Heat to boil while stirring frequently. Lower heat to medium. Simmer for 40 minutes while stirring continuously. Pour in dishes and let cool. Refrigerate. Sprinkle coconut, almonds and pine nuts on top.

Time of preparation: 5 minutes
Time of cooking: 55 minutes

Desserts and Beverages

Ashta Substitute
(ashta)

Yields 28 ounces | 770 calories per serving

4 cups	whole milk
2 tablespoons	semolina
4 tablespoons	corn starch
2 tablespoons	orange blossom water

Place milk in a heavy pan. Heat to boil. Stir well while
heating. Lower heat to simmer. Add semolina, corn starch
and orange blossom water. While simmering stir continuously
until a thick pudding-like mixture is formed. Pour mix in
a large pan. Let cool in refrigerator. Ashta substitute is used
as a filling for some Arabic sweets.

Time of cooking: 25 minutes

Ashta Rolls
(znoud al sit)

SERVES 15 | 242 calories per serving
(2 pieces per serving)

12 ounces	fillo dough
1/2 cup	unsalted butter
1 recipe	ashta substitute (page 142)
1 recipe	basic syrup (page 128)
1/4 cup	finely ground pistachio nuts

Cut fillo dough into 6x6 inch squares Brush the top of 2 or 3 sheets of fillo dough with butter. Place 1 tablespoon ashta in the middle of the sheet. Fold both edges of sheet toward the center then roll firmly into a cylinder. Brush top with butter and place on a greased baking sheet. Bake cylinders until bottom is golden brown (approximately 30-40 minutes). Remove from oven and pour 2-3 tablespoon of basic syrup over each piece. Let cool at room temperature and sprinkle pistachio over rolls.

Time of preparation: 60 minutes
Time of cooking: 40 minutes

Hlawee with Cheese
(Hlawee al jibin)

SERVES 15 | 212 calories per serving

2 pounds	unsalted cheese curds or Ricotta cheese
1 1/4 cups	semolina
1/2 recipe	basic syrup (page 128)
	(add rose water to basic syrup)
2 pounds	ashta
1/2 cup	finely minced pistachios

Melt the cheese in a double boiler. Stir cheese as it is melting.
Add semolina and 1 cup of basic syrup recipe and stir well as
mixture is heated. Spread mixture evenly in a 10x15 inch pan
to 1/4 inch thickness. Cut into 3 inches squares. Place ashta
in a row in the middle of each square and roll square
in a cylinder shape. Sprinkle pistachios on top.

Time of preparation: 5 minutes
Time of cooking: 15 minutes

Amhiyyi
(amhiyyi)

SERVES 5

1 cup	whole wheat kernels rinsed and drained
1/4 cup	anise seeds
	sugar
	raisins
	walnuts, chopped
	orange blossom water
	Sweet pomegranate seeds

Place whole wheat kernels and anise seeds in a pan. Cover with water. Heat to boil. Simmer under medium heat until tender (approximately 90 minutes). Wheat kernels are then poured in individual cups just prior to serving. Add, as desired, sugar, raisins, walnuts, pomegranate seeds, and 1 or 2 drops of orange blossom water. Served in Lebanon when a baby's first tooth appears.

Time of preparation: 5 minutes
Time of cooking: 90 minutes

Knafi with Cheese
(knafi bil jibin)

SERVES 8 | 509 calories per serving

1 pound	shredded fillo dough (or knafi dough)
1 cup	unsalted and melted butter
16 ounces	unsalted cheese curds or Ricotta cheese
1 1/2 cups	basic syrup (page 128)

Break shredded phyllo dough apart and place in a bowl. Pour melted butter on top and mix well. Spread half dough over the bottom of a 9 x12 inch pan. Place cheese evenly over the bottom layer of the knafi dough. Cover cheese evenly with the remaining dough. Bake in a preheated oven at 350°F until bottom is golden brown. Broil for 1 minute until top is light brown. Remove from oven and immediately pour syrup over knafi. Serve while warm.

Time of preparation: 15 minutes
Time of cooking: 45 minutes to 1 hour

Arabic Coffee
(ahwee)

SERVES 2

2 demitasse cups	water
2 tablespoons	fine ground coffee (Arabic coffee)
	Sugar

Place water in a coffee pot (called raqwi). Heat to boil.
Remove raqwi from fire. Add coffee to hot water with
desired sugar and stir well. Coffee is then brought to boil
under light fire 3 or 4 times, removing each time from fire
to allow foam to recede. To prevent spillage of coffee, it
is important to remove immediately as foam starts to rise.
Coffee is then allowed to rest for few minutes prior to serving.
Arabic coffee might be flavored with one drop of orange
blossom water per demitasse cup or with cardamom powder
usually boiled with coffee.

Time of preparation/cooking: 7 minutes

White Coffee
(ahwee bayda)

SERVES 2

2 cups	water
1 teaspoon	orange blossom water
	sugar (optional)

Heat water to boil. Add orange blossom to hot water.
Serve with sugar.

Anise Tea
(shay yansoun)

SERVES 2

2 1/2 cups	water
1 tablespoon	anise seeds
	sugar

Heat water to boil. Add anise seeds and boil for 2 more minutes. Strain in serving cups. Serve with sugar.

Desserts and Beverages

Sauces & Condiments

Tahini with Lemon
(taratour)

Makes 8.4 Ounces | 816 Calories per recipe

2 cloves	garlic
1/4 teaspoon	salt
1/2 cup	lemon juice
1/2 cup	tahini
1/2 cup	water
1/4 cup	finely chopped parsley leaves or
	1/2 tablespoon dried and minced
	parsley leaves

Crush garlic with salt. In a blender place garlic, lemon juice, tahini, water and mix well. Place tahini mixture in a bowl. Add parsley and stir well with a spoon.

Estimated time of preparation: 10 minutes

Garlic & Oil
(zayt bil toum)

Makes 5.8 Ounces | 588 Calories per recipe

8 cloves	garlic
1/2 teaspoon	salt
1/2 cup	olive oil
1/4 cup	fresh lemon juice

Mash garlic with salt. Add oil slowly while stirring well.
Add lemon juice and mix well. Used to baste or marinate
chicken or meat. Can be stored in the freezer.

Estimated time of preparation: 10 minutes

Fish Hot Sauce
(sauce samak Har)

Makes 25 Ounces | 3947 Calories per recipe

10 cloves	garlic
1/2 teaspoon	salt
1 bunch	green cilantro
1/2 cup	vegetable oil
3/4 pound	walnuts finely processed
1 recipe	Tahini with Lemon (page)

Mash garlic, salt and cilantro well. Sauté in oil for 2-3
minutes. Add walnut and sauté further for 2 more minutes.
Add taratour and mix well under low heat until oil is mixed
well with taratour. Pour on baked fish.

Estimated time of preparation: 30 minutes

White Sauce
(sauce bayda)

Makes 28 Ounces | 616 Calories per recipe

2 tablespoons	flour
2 tablespoons	butter
1 teaspoon	salt
1 cup	milk

In a pan sauté flour with butter for 2-3 minutes. Add salt and milk slowly while stirring continuously. Heat to boil then simmer under low to medium heat while stirring continuously for approximately 20 minutes.

Estimated time of preparation: 25 minutes

Pickled Eggplant
(batinjan makbous)

169 Calories per eggplant

4 pounds	small eggplants (4-5 inches in length), ends snipped (approximately 12)
8 ounces	finely diced walnuts
1 tablespoon	salt, divided
20 cloves	garlic, finely diced
2 large	green peppers, finely diced
1	jalapeño pepper (optional)

Pickling Liqued: (this amount is dependent on you jar sizes)
1 cup vinegar and 2 tablespoons salt for every 2 cups of water

1/4 cup olive oil

Place eggplants in a pan and cover with water. Heat to boil.
Simmer for approximately 15 minutes. Remove eggplant
from heat and place in a strainer under cold running water.
A 2-inch slit is then made in the middle of each eggplant.
Prepare eggplants filling by mixing walnuts, 1 tablespoon
salt, garlic, green pepper and jalapeño well. Fill each
eggplant with filling and place in a sterile glass container.
Cover eggplant with pickling liquid (1/2 cup vinegar and
2 tablespoon salt for every 2 cups of water). Pour olive oil
on top of pickling solution. Store pickled eggplant at room
temperature. It will be ready to eat in 4-5 days.

Estimated time of preparation: 30 minutes

Pickled Turnip
(lift makbous)

41 Calories per turnip

   4 pounds   whole turnips, cut into bite size pieces

Pickling Liqued: (this amount is dependent on you jar sizes)
1 cup vinegar and 2 tablespoons salt for every 2 cups of water

   1   root beet sliced into 5 pieces
1 tablespoon   bread crumbs

Place turnips in a sterile glass container. Cover with pickling liquid. Add root beet slices and bread crumbs to container (root beet colors the turnips into pink). Cover and allow 5 days for pickling to occur.

Estimated time of preparation: 25 minutes

Pickled Stuffed Sweet Pepper
(flayfle makbouse)

88 Calories per stuffed green pepper

2 pounds	cabbage, finely chopped
1 pound	carrots thinly sliced
15 cloves	garlic, mashed
20	dark olives, seeds removed
1	jalapeño pepper (optional)
1/2 cup	olive oil
1 tablespoon	salt
10 large	green peppers

Pickling Liqued: (this amount is dependent on you jar sizes)
1 cup vinegar and 2 tablespoons salt for every 2 cups of water

Prepare filling by mixing cabbage, carrots, garlic, olives, jalapeño pepper, oil and 1 tablespoon salt well. Stuff green peppers with filling. Place in a sterile glass container. Cover with pickling liquid. Close container and allow 5 days for pickling to occur.

Estimated time of preparation: 25 minutes

Pickled Cucumber
(khyar makbous)

48 Calories per cucumber

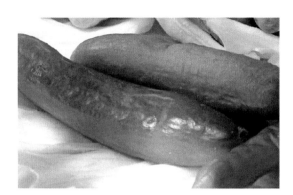

2 pounds	small cucumbers (4-5 inches long) approximately 14
5 whole	cloves garlic

Pickling Liqued: (this amount is dependent on you jar sizes)
1 cup vinegar and 2 tablespoons salt for every 2 cups of water

Place cucumber and whole cloves of garlic in a sterile glass container. Cover cucumber with pickling liquid. Cover and allow 5 days for pickling to occur.

Estimated time of preparation: 10 minutes

Menu Planning

Appetizers

Appetizers or mezza in Lebanon can be an overwhelming experience. Up to 60 different small dishes (21 of which is listed below) might be served prior to the main meal. It is a ritual that extended family and friends enjoy for hours. Mezza is commonly served with "arak", a Lebanese spirit.

Non-Vegetarian Menu

Menu 1

Menu 2

Menu 3

Menu 4

Vegetarian Menu

Menu 1

Menu 2

Menu 3

Menu 4

Glossary

Helpful Cooking Terms

Baste:	to moisten food during cooking with a liquid
Blanch:	to soak into hot or boiling water for a brief period of time
Broil:	to cook by exposing to direct intense heat
Chop:	to cut into small pieces of irregular sizes
Cube:	to cut into 1/2-inch or larger cubes
Dash:	small amount of an ingredient usually not exceeding 1/8 of a teaspoon
Dice:	to cut into small cubes (less than 1/2 inch)
Grate:	to mince into fine pieces using the small holes of a grater
Lukewarm:	moderately warm temperature (approximately 98o F)
Marinate:	to soak in marinade for several hours
Mince:	finely chop into very small particles
Parboil:	to simmer until food is almost cooked
Peel:	to strip off the outer skin or covering with the fingers
Sauté:	to fry quickly in little fat while stirring frequently
Shred:	to cut into long narrow pieces using a knife or the large holes of a shredder
Simmer:	to boil gently at or just below boiling point
Skim:	to remove foam from the top surface of a liquid
Slice:	to cut into thin flat pieces
Snip:	to cut into small pieces with scissors using quick short strokes
Tear:	to separate into pieces with fingers

Measuring Ingredients

You can measure ingredients by using the following:

1. **Graduated measuring spoons**. These can be used for liquids and dry ingredients. Different sizes include: 1/4 teaspoon, 1/2 teaspoon, 1 teaspoon and 1 tablespoon.

2. **Graduated nested measuring cups**: These are primarily used for dry ingredients and solid fats. Different sizes include: 1/4 cup, 1/3 cup, 1/2 cup, 3/4 cup and 1 cup.

3. **Glass measuring cup**: used to measure liquids. Measurements need to be done at eye level. Reading can be in fluid ounces (fl.oz) or milliliters (ml).

EQUIVALENT MEASURES

Dry measures

1 pound (pd) = 16.23 ounces (oz) = 454.54 grams = 0.45 kilograms
1 ounce = 28 grams
1 gram = 0.0357 ounce

Liquid measures

1 tablespoon (tbsp.) = 3 teaspoons (tsp.)
2 cups = 1 pint
2 pints = 1 quart
4 quarts = 1 gallon

cups	tbsp.	ml	fl.oz
1/16	1	15	1/2
1/4	4	60	2
1/3	5 1/3	80	2.7
1/2	8	120	4
3/4	12	180	6
1	16	240	8
2	32	480	16

APPROXIMATE MEASURES

1 cup	weight (grams)
Burghul	170
Flour	140
Lentils	200
Lima beans	200
Garbanzo beans	200
Sugar	190
Fava beans	200
Coriander	105
kishek	180
Walnuts	120
Pine nuts	140
krawyat	130
Sumac	100
Rice	180
Vermicelli	60
Pistachio	125
Sesame	145
Dried Thyme	80
Za'tar	140

FRESH VEGETABLES

Chopped tomato	170 (1 large)
Sliced cucumber	140 (1/2 large)
Sliced carrot	150 (2 large)
Sliced zucchini	130 (1 small)
Diced potato	180 (1 medium)
Chopped onion	120 (1 large)
Torn lettuce	50
Green bean	105
Parsley	25
Celery	105
Broccoli	75
Cauliflower	110
Chopped green pepper	100
Green peas	130

MISCELLANEOUS

Yogurt	140
Basic syrup	300

English-Lebanese Cooking Terms

Appetizers....................mezza

Beans.............................lubieh

Bread...............................khubz

Cabbage....................malfouf

Cauliflower.............arnabeet

Cheese..............................jibin

Chick peas...............Hommus

Chicken...........................djaj

Coffee...........................ahwee

Crushed wheat...........burghul

Cucumber.....................khyar

Dough.............................ajeen

Drinks..........................sharab

Eggplant....................batinjan

Eggs.................................bayd

Fig...................................teen

Fish.................................samak

Fried..............................meqlee

Garbanzo...........see chick peas

Garlic.............................toum

Grape leaves.........waraq einab

Ice cream......................bouza

Lentils............................adas

Meat................................laHm

Okra................................bami

Olives.........................zaytoun

Omelet...............................ijji

Parsley....................baqdounis

Peppers............................bhar

Potato............................batata

Poultry.................see chicken

Rice.....................................riz

Salads............................slatet

Soups..........................shurbat

Spinach......................sbanigh

Stuffed meals.............meHshi

Sweets............................Helou

Swiss chard....................seliq

Tea..................................shay

Thyme...........................za'tar

Tomato..................banadoura

Turnips.............................lifit

Wheat............................ameH

Yogurt............................laban

Zucchini........................kousa

Lebanese-English Cooking Terms

Adas	lentils	**Laban**	yogurt
Ahwee	coffee	**Labni**	yogurt spread
Ajeen	dough	**LaHm**	meat
AmeH	wheat	**Lifit**	turnips
Arnabeet	cauliflower	**Lubieh**	beans
Bami	okra	**Macaroni**	pasta
Banadoura	tomato	**Malfouf**	cabbage
Baqdounis	parsley	**MeHshi**	stuffed
Batata	potato	**Meqlee**	fried
Batinjan	eggplant	**Mezza**	appetizers
Bayd	eggs	**Mighli**	rice pudding
Bhar	pepper	**Mnaqeesh**	pizza
Bouza	ice cream	**Nkha't**	brains
Burghul	crushed wheat	**Qasbi**	liver
Djaj	chicken	**Riz**	rice
Fatoush	bread salad	**Rqaqat**	fillo dough
Fasoulia	beans	**Salsa**	sauce
Fasoulia bayda	lima beans	**Samak**	fish
Fasoulia Hamra	red beans	**Sbanigh**	spinach
Foul	fava beans	**Seliq**	Swiss chard
Fwaki	fruit	**Sharab**	drinks
Ftayer	pie	**Shay**	tea
Habash	turkey	**Shurbat**	soup
Halib	milk	**Slatet**	salad
Hamoud	lemon	**Bazela**	sweet peas
Hommus	chick peas	**Teen**	fig
Ijji	omelet	**Toum**	garlic
Jibin	cheese	**Waraq einab**	grape leaves
Khubz	bread	**Zayt**	oil
Khudra	vegetable	**Zaytoun**	olives
Khyar	cucumber	**Za'tar**	thyme
Kishek	crushed wheat & yogurt		
Kousa	zucchini		

Calories & Nutrition Chart
(per serving)

FOOD SELECTION	CALORIES (Cal)	CHO (gm)	Prot (gm)	Fat (gm)	SAT. FAT (gm)	Cholesterol (mg)
BREAD						
Basic bread dough	264	55	7	1	0	0
Pie dough	429	55	8	20	3	0
Meat Pizza	571	58	20	29	7	31
Za'tar pizza	517	55	8	30	4	0
Cheese pizza	593	56	19	32	10	44
Spinach pie	335	33	8	20	3	0
Kishek Pie	358	47	11	14	-	7
Egg pie	583	56	20	31	6	517
Meat pie	203	14	4	15	2	6
Meat-stuffed fillo dough	84	6	4	5	2	14
SALAD						
Tabouli	409	16	3	38	5	0
Yogurt and cucumber	160	17	10	6	2	23
Potato salad	209	24	6	10	2	155
Green thyme salad	213	10	2	19	2	0
Bread salad	306	19	5	25	3	0
Mixed vegetables salad	135	7	2	12	1	0
Swiss chard with tahini	213	8	7	17	3	0
Lima bean salad	426	33	10	29	4	0
Root beet and cabbage salad	133	12	2	10	1	0
Green bean salad	200	17	4	14	3	0
Potato salad with tahini	402	52	8	9	3	0
SOUPS						
Vegetable and meat soup	136	14	13	3	2	34
Vegetable and chicken soup	110	12	12	1	0	29
Rice and meat soup	243	14	37	29	6	83
Rice and chicken soup	273	14	41	4	1	133
Lentils soup	404	39	11	23	3	0
Meatball soup	243	12	24	10	6	70
Crushed wheat and yogurt soup	273	20	23	11	9	59
Tomato and onion soup	78	11	24	4	1	0
Lentils and Swiss chard soup	363	43	13	17	2	0
Lentils and dough pie soup	442	46	13	23	4	0
Mixed grains soup	338	32	9	20	3	0
YOGURT						
Basic yogurt	113	11	7	4	3	17
Yogurt spread	70	7	5	3	2	10
Labni preserved balls	147	7	5	11	3	10
Yogurt and garbanzo beans	501	70	24	15	7	19
Stuffed zucchini and yogurt	423	50	31	12	6	99
Kibbi with yogurt	437	62	28	9	3	86
Beef with yogurt	445	48	40	10	8	135
Meat stuffed pastries with yogurt	490	61	33	12	8	113

Flavors of Lebanon

FOOD SELECTION	CALORIES (Cal)	CHO (gm)	Prot (gm)	Fat (gm)	SAT. FAT (gm)	Cholesterol (mg)
MEAT						
Lebanese Hamburger	230	2	35	8	4	104
Baked Kafta with potatoe	422	29	50	11	7	140
Raw Kibbi	366	40	30	10	4	72
Cooked kibbi (stuffed)	620	50	45	28	12	120
Kibbi Stuffing	176	3	14	13	3	36
Kibbi and kishek	383	46	22	12	-	45
Green bean meat stew	199	8	19	10	5	52
Okra meat stew	498	12	26	39	10	70
Sweet peas meat stew	264	15	26	10	1	69
Stuffed grape leaves	336	38	22	9	5	52
White bean meat stew	419	42	38	11	6	69
Meat roll with eggs	597	8	47	40	17	387
Burghul with meat	382	45	29	9	6	68
Fried meat with bread crumbs	498	15	45	29	12	232
Stuffed egplant and zucchini	444	38	23	24	9	54
Beef tenderloin and vegetables	531	20	59	22	10	192
Meat and vegetables dish	280	22	23	11	4	60
Meat balls and rice	448	5	43	30	14	128
Artichokes and meat	190	17	12	10	3	24
Spinach meat stew	307	13	31	18	7	64
Rice and meat	520	45	29	25	8	77
Green fava bean meat stew	379	51	24	9	3	42
Meat-stuffed eggplants	496	27	19	38	8	38
Baked eggplant and zucchini	278	22	27	10	4	70
POULTRY						
Baked Chicken and vegetable	412	17	50	15	3	130
Chicken and rice	610	53	51	21	6	123
Pasta and chicken with white sauce	510	38	57	14	6	187
Burghul with chicken	462	46	30	17	3	59
Moghrabieh with chicken	661	72	61	14	2	120
Barbecued chicken	403	2	44	23	4	118
Chicken and bread crumbs	506	26	53	20	4	326
Stuffed chicken	891	14	90	51	13	336
Mlukhiyyi with chicken	540	57	48	12	5	104
Chicken with curry	666	50	64	22	9	159
Stuffed turkey	845	14	99	41	10	327
Chicken with white sauce	647	12	37	19	3	82
Chicken and wheat kernels	476	8	71	16	7	198

FOOD SELECTION	CALORIES (Cal)	CHO (gm)	Prot (gm)	Fat (gm)	SAT. FAT (gm)	Cholesterol (mg)
SAUCES AND CONDIMENTS						
Tahini with lemon (8.4 oz)	816	24	25	29	10	0
Garlic with oil (5.8 oz)	588	21	3	57	7	0
Fish hot sauce (25 oz)	3946	74	110	379	37	0
White sauce (28 oz)	616	64	34	25	4	16
Pickled eggplant (per eggplant)	169	15	5	12	1	0
Pickled turnip (per turnip)	41	9	1	0	0	0
Pickled sweet pepper (per pepper)	90	16	3	2	0	0
Pickled cucumber (per cucumber)	48	12	1	0	0	0

FOOD SELECTION	CALORIES (Cal)	CHO (gm)	Prot (gm)	Fat (gm)	SAT. FAT (gm)	Cholesterol (mg)
FISH DISHES						
Fish and rice	824	62	40	46	7	77
Fish and onion	642	8	38	51	7	77
Baked fish in hot sauce	684	10	65	43	6	138
Fried fish	762	48	55	39	6	92
Fish in kibbi	489	34	31	26	4	57
Shrimp in avocado	771	38	18	65	-	109
VEGETARIAN DISHES						
Lebanese omelet	305	13	10	24	3	355
Rice Pilaf	198	38	3	3	1	0
Chick peas dip	224	26	11	9	1	0
Rice and curry	235	45	6	3	1	0
Green Bean Stew	225	13	3	19	2	0
Lentils with rice	453	56	15	20	3	0
Fava beans with lemon juice	305	32	13	15	2	0
Roasted Cauliflower	240	15	6	19	2	0
Kibbet raheb	557	61	15	29	4	0
Baked eggplant with tahini	186	12	5	14	2	0
Baked eggplant	82	10	2	5	1	0
Green okra with tomato	414	17	1	38	5	0
Falafel	414	20	8	35	5	0
Lentils with burghul	446	53	17	20	2	0
Drained lentils	456	54	18	20	2	0
Stuffed Swiss chard leaves	330	41	6	17	2	0
Cooked red beans	403	43	16	20	2	0
Stuffed grape leaves	306	40	4	14	2	0
Spaghetti in white sauce	382	49	18	12	5	28
DESSERTS AND BEVERAGES						
Basic syrup recipe (1 cup)	372	96	0	0	0	0
Ma'moul with semolina	288	44	6	10	6	26
Ma'moul with walnuts	447	53	9	24	8	30
Awwaymat sweet	237	24	1	15	2	0
Semolina squares	255	41	5	8	4	18
Baklava	192	18	3	13	5	18
Ka'k	220	40	5	4	2	47
Butter cookies	150	17	2	8	5	21
Caramel cream	192	30	7	5	2	192
Rice pudding with milk	314	57	7	7	2	7
Mhallabieh	326	72	5	2	1	8
Ashtalieh	363	84	4	2	1	8
Baked suzettes with filling	433	93	6	5	1	44
Spiced rice pudding	345	69	3	7	-	0
Ashta substitute (28 oz)	770	92	33	30	18	123
Ashta rolls	242	34	5	10	5	25
Hlawee with cheese	212	26	16	5	2	14
Knafi with cheese	509	56	15	24	15	66

Index

Flavors of Lebanon